SS GREAT
BRITAIN

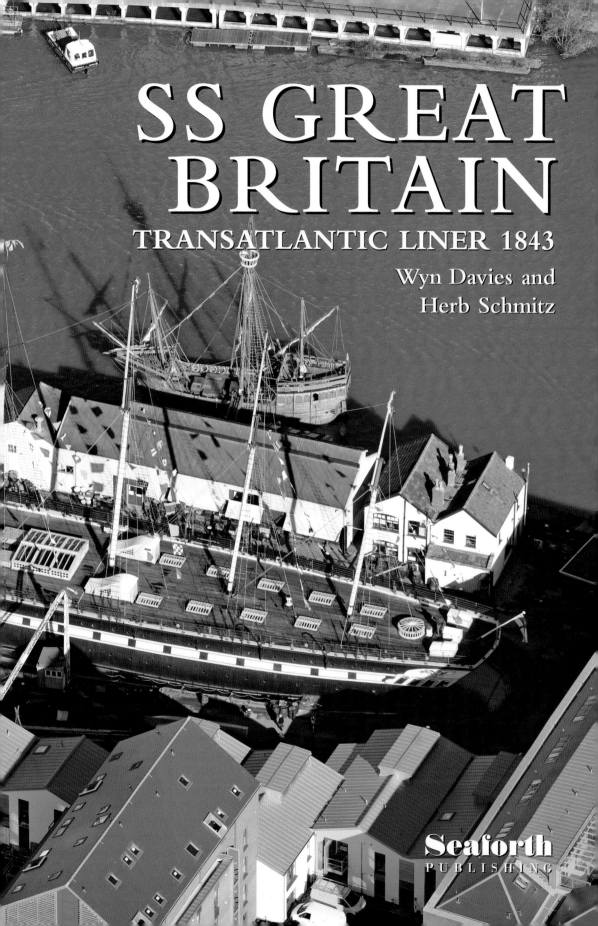

SS GREAT BRITAIN
TRANSATLANTIC LINER 1843

Wyn Davies and
Herb Schmitz

Seaforth
PUBLISHING

Copyright © Wyn Davies & Herb Schmitz 2012

First published in Great Britain in 2012 by
Seaforth Publishing, Pen & Sword Books Ltd,
47 Church Street, Barnsley S70 2AS

Reprinted 2017

www.seaforthpublishing.com

British Library Cataloguing in Publication Data

A catalogue record for this book is available from the
British Library

ISBN 978 1 84832 144 1

The right of Wyn Davies and Herb Schmitz to be
identified as the authors of this work has been asserted
by them in accordance with the Copyright, Designs and
Patents Act 1988.

Art Direction and Design by Stephen Dent
Deck layouts by Tony Garrett
Printed and bound in China by
1010 Printing International Ltd.

CONTENTS

Half title: SS *Great Britain* 'afloat' in the original dock where she was built.

Title pages: The huge iron hull dwarfs the replica of the *Matthew*, the fifteenth-century caravel, built to celebrate the 500th anniversary of Cabot's voyage to Newfoundland in 1497. *(The SS Great Britain Trust)*

Above left: The promenade saloon, now perfectly restored, where first-class passengers once exercised and socialised, away from the wind and spray of the weather deck.

Following pages: *Great Britain* faces out of what was originally the Great Western Dock, towards the Bristol docks. This is what she would have looked like, dressed overall in signal flags, on her launch in 1843 when she was floated out.

THE SS *GREAT BRITAIN* IS AN EXTRAORDINARY
survivor from an age of invention and aspiration. She symbolises the inventiveness of Brunel and his collaborators who dared to develop new ideas in engineering and transform the future for world travel. She represents the aspiration of thousands of passengers who travelled the world, taking advantage of a revolution in global communication.

The ss *Great Britain*'s story is one of transformation, as well as survival. Her innovative design, combining the technologies of iron construction and a steam-powered propeller, made her the prototype of virtually all modern ships. In 1843, when she was launched, public opinion was divided between scepticism and optimism; some doubted that an iron ship of this size would even float, let along make it across the Atlantic. In the event, her success forced the pace of change, so that within forty years she was – although still sound and serviceable – overtaken by a new generation of iron- and later steel-built passenger steamers.

The ss *Great Britain* was built to take advantage of a commercial opportunity, not as a test piece. Her first voyages, carrying passengers between Liverpool and New York, were fraught with technical problems affecting the propeller machinery. Commercial operation meant that these, and other design issues, had to be resolved quickly. Brunel's basic concept was soon modified, with development of the engines, the rig and the propeller, to create a vessel which really could go the distance. By the end of her working life, the ss *Great Britain* had sailed thirty-two times around the world, visited five continents, and travelled nearly a million miles at sea.

Today the ss Great Britain Trust seeks to sustain the inspiration this ship represents. Since 1970, when a heroic salvage brought her home to the drydock in which she was built, millions of people have visited her. The Trust invests not just in conserving the ship, but in offering all of these visitors an authentic and exciting experience of the history she represents. Conserved in her building dock, and surrounded by a glass 'sea', the ss *Great Britain* appears ready to set off on her journey once again, carrying today's visitors with her on a new adventure.

As a souvenir of such a visit, this book offers an informed and accessible account of the ship's history, generously illustrated with views of the reconstructed interiors and historic source material. The Trust welcomes this addition to the growing range of works on the ss *Great Britain* and her creator, Isambard Kingdom Brunel.

Dr Kate Rambridge,
ss Great Britain Trust
April 2012

BRUNEL'S
ss GREAT BRITAIN™

1 | INTRODUCTION

SOMEONE VISITING BRISTOL DOCKS TODAY for the first time in, say, ten years would find it hard to recognise the surroundings, such is the pace of change today; how much harder then would it be for the ghost of a certain Isambard Kingdom Brunel, returning after nearly 200 years to the city he did so much to promote. He might recognise some of Temple Meads railway station, and he would certainly still be able to see his suspension bridge, but were he to catch a glimpse of masts through the many new blocks of offices and flats, he would surely be a little mystified to find his other famous Bristol creation, the SS *Great Britain*, back in its original berth. Unique amongst heritage vessels preserved in Britain, the *Great Britain* has been restored and opened to an admiring public on the very spot where she was built.

The largest ship in the world at her launch, built of a material many believed untried, and powered by the still relatively novel steam engine, it was typical of Brunel's approach to things that she incorporated several firsts into her design.

Modern engineers are often encouraged to minimise or even eradicate untried features if they wish their

Great Britain's career began in 1843 and lasted until her abandonment in Sparrow Cove in the Falkland Islands in 1937, her internal decking having been removed to build a jetty at Port Stanley. In ninety years she underwent many modifications, and she is depicted here in 1846, her original six-masted schooner rig having been reduced to five masts to improve her balance. *(The SS Great Britain Trust)*

project to succeed. Brunel would have none of this timidity. Perhaps fortunately, he was nearly always right and just as often had the force of character to get his proposals accepted. Equally, he was occasionally just that bit too far ahead of his time, and self-induced stress may have contributed to his early death during the building of his next ship, the *Great Eastern*.

In this book we will attempt to show that Brunel's approach to the design of the *Great Britain*, whilst forward-looking, was still within the realms of what was possible with Britain's growing industrial capabilities, and that his thinking was definitely more clear-sighted than many of his contemporaries, although he still needed his powers of persuasion from time to time. The result was a vessel which was a world beater at her launch.

2 | BACKGROUND

ON STARTING THE RESEARCH FOR THIS BOOK
there was an assumption that the design, build and
career of *Great Britain* would be quite different to that
of HMS *Warrior*, the author's previous project.
However, as the research progressed the more the simi-
larities came out. Both vessels were pioneers in their
field; both relied on the growing maturity of steam
propulsion and iron manufacture; both were the largest
of their type; both spent relatively little time at the task
for which they were designed, and spent the majority
of their service lives in a secondary role (perhaps
stretching the analogy a bit as the *Great Britain* was
very successful in her Australian role); both were
hulked and both rescued from oblivion in the same
decade. Of course, the *Great Britain* was the older of
the two, by almost twenty years in conception and
fifteen by launch date, so can perhaps lay greater claim
to being a pioneer.

Another parallel was that both ships were, in part,
conceived to overcome a threat to the country's
primacy from overseas. In the case of the *Great Britain*
this was as a response to the winning of the bulk of
the transatlantic passenger and mail trade by
American packet boats. Their speed and relative relia-
bility had drawn wealthy passengers away from the
British merchant marine for some time, in an era when
Britannia expected to be predominant. It took the
Americans to produce the agency of their own down-
fall when their civil war led to the flight of their
merchant ships to the British flag for protection
against the depredations of Confederate commerce
raiders, themselves mainly built in Britain! A situation
from which, despite the enormous building
programmes of the Second World War, they never
fully recovered.

Returning to the *Great Britain*, the pioneering Great
Western Railway had already been persuaded, probably
mainly by Brunel, to in effect extend the railway from
Bristol to New York by steamship. To this end the
SS *Great Western* was commissioned from Brunel and
put into service in 1837, whilst at the same time a
sister-ship was being considered.

Like the *Great Britain*, the *Great Western* was built
in Bristol, at the yard of William Patterson at
Wapping, near the now home of the Bristol M-Shed
Museum. Interestingly, the name Wapping seems to
have migrated west along Spike Island as the Great
Western Dock became known as the Wapping Wharf
at some stage in its history. The *Great Western's* struc-
ture illustrated Brunel's striving for a long life for his
creations. By standards then current, her structure

more nearly reflects that of a warship than a merchant
ship. Her framing was built up from futtocks (pieces
of heavy timber) and bolted in pairs, but Brunel went
further and bolted each pair directly together and
then in larger groups along the whole length of the
ship. This structure was caulked and made watertight
before any of the actual planking was added. Such
strength of structure was probably seen by Brunel as
necessary to carry the vibration loads of a steam
engine, and may have owed something to his contin-
uing links with the Admiralty at the time, with the
Surveyor's office offering help and advice during the
Great Western's design.

Upon this immensely strong foundation were
mounted the engines, from Maudsley, Son and Field,
continuing Brunel's longstanding relationship with
them, although his assessment of the engine tenders
and the final selection of Maudsley is a model of disin-
terest whilst admitting his relationship with the
company. These engines drove two 28ft 9in (8.75m)
diameter paddle wheels, which had to be installed on
the Thames as they wouldn't have fitted through
Bristol's dock gates.

Despite being the largest of her type at her launch,

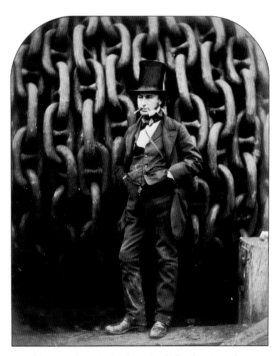

A well-known photograph of Isambard Kingdom Brunel,
standing before the launch chains of the *Great Eastern*, with his
trademark stovepipe hat and cigar. *(The SS Great Britain Trust)*

On her first crossing of the Atlantic, *Great Western* arrived off New York on 23 April 1838 after a crossing of 15 days 12 hours (averaging 8.66 knots), thus beating the time of *Sirius*, the first steamship to carry passengers across the Atlantic, which had arrived only hours earlier. She can arguably be regarded as the first winner of the Blue Riband, the mythical and unofficial trophy for the fastest ship on the Atlantic. *(The SS Great Britain Trust)*

the *Great Western* was in effect a relatively standard-outline paddle steamer and can be considered as a representative of a previous generation with her wooden structure. A few quick sums would show a modern naval architect that this wooden structure occupied some 36,700cu ft (just over 1000m³), most of which was lost cargo volume when compared with an iron-built ship. If we take the finding that *Great Britain*'s structure accounted for a quarter of her displacement and take the displacement of *Great Western* at 10ft draught as 1200 tons, an equivalent iron hull would weigh 300 tons or 305 tonnes and take up just 41m³. Obviously this is rather simplistic, but it clearly illustrates the advantage of iron over wood, which rapidly became apparent to shippers and shipowners alike.

At this stage, the propulsion of the second ship was to have followed that of the *Great Western* and been by paddle wheel. Two things then occurred that almost certainly had a significant bearing on events. One was the visit to Bristol of the *Archimedes*, a screw propeller ship. Constructed by the Ship Propeller Company to demonstrate the virtues of screw propulsion, she was on a round-Britain voyage to test the propeller in service conditions. The Great Western Steamship Company (GWSC) directors borrowed her for some trials of their own, the results of which caused the building committee to decide to halt the paddle steamer design and get Brunel to prepare a report on

the feasibility of using a propeller. At around the same time the Admiralty were to trial the propeller and had engaged Brunel as consultant. This led to the design and construction of HMS *Rattler*, of which more later.

Having satisfied himself of the economics of a steam-powered transatlantic service, Brunel had also proved to his satisfaction the economies of scale, that larger ships took less power for the same speed than simple scaling up all round would suggest. He was to take this to an apparent extreme with the *Great Eastern*, but as a first step the running mate to the *Great Western* was his next concern.

As will be described later, this project went through several turns of the design spiral before emerging as the *Great Britain*. The largest ship in the world at the time of her launch and for some time afterwards, she was constructed throughout of iron and powered by steam-driven screw propeller, a combination that set the precedent for the next hundred years, although steel eventually replaced iron for the main structure.

THE MERCHANT MARINE

To the modern reader the fact that British shipping once carried the bulk of world trade may come as something of a surprise. Not only did Britain supply the bulk of the shipping, but it also built the majority of the world's ships, merchant or naval. This state of affairs was very much in embryo when Brunel was at work in Bristol, but what he started would last until the major losses of two World Wars finally unseated Britannia, in somewhat less time than it took to establish the position in the first place.

Whilst ships were built out of wood, anyone with a handy forest could do the job. Once the economies of using iron and later steel became apparent to the shippers, it was only those countries with a sufficiently developed industrial infrastructure which could build enough ships to meet the demand, and that was mainly Britain for almost the whole of the nineteenth and the start of the twentieth century.

For much of English, and later British, history, shipping routes were the jealously guarded secrets of the then dominant powers; first Portugal, then Spain and then the Dutch. By the time Drake made his much publicised voyage round the world, Spain had already established shipping routes to and from the Far East, and across the Pacific to California and Mexico for onward shipment to Spain across the Atlantic. Most of Drake's contemporaries spent their time trying to break through this protectionism, by fair means or foul, which is why they were very much regarded as pirates by the Spanish.

Protectionism was very much the name of the game, though, and in common with its rivals England passed several Navigation Acts designed to ensure that English goods were carried in English bottoms.[1] Such acts are first recorded in England in 1381 and the last was finally rescinded in 1834. Elsewhere some still survive to this day, the most notable being the Jones Act in force in US coastal waters.

In Britain's case the acts served to help develop a merchant fleet which grew with the number of overseas colonies and markets, although in the long run such protectionism tended to stifle developments in ship design. Outside competition can then serve to highlight this lack of development and this seems to have been particularly true of the North Atlantic. Skilful design and construction of ships had long been a forte of Britain's North American colonies and had served as their weapon against our restrictive practices, a weapon that became a real commercial threat once the colonies gained their independence. Fast, well-designed American ships could and did outrun not just the Royal Navy, but also Britain's merchant fleets, making profitable voyages throughout the wars with France, for example. However, in some cases it seems a blind eye was turned to breaking the rules because Wellington, for one, was very clear that the survival of his army on the Spanish Peninsula depended on supplies from America arriving in American ships.

Building on these skills, in 1817 the United States introduced the first transatlantic passenger and mail packets,[2] swift little ships that were the start of a regular and fairly reliable service which quickly made inroads into the market, eventually driving British ships off the route almost totally. It must be emphasised that the key word here is regular. A scheduled service allowed shippers to know exactly when to expect their goods, passengers to know when they would be arriving or on what date they would be sailing, and the American ships ran to a timetable, perhaps for the first time in maritime history outside of river traffic.

It was against this background that the first tentative steps were taken to introduce steam to deep sea crossings. The first Admiralty-designed steamship, the *Comet*, was launched at Woolwich Dockyard in 1821, and the East India Company had carried out trials as early as 1816; their *Diana* was probably the first steamship to see action, in 1824, during an expedition to Burma. In the same year the Admiralty purchased six steamships for the navy, some two years ahead of Abney-Hasting's *Karteria* of Greek War of Independence fame. Links between the Royal Navy and the major commercial operators were always good, and Hastings, for example, was ex-Royal Navy so it is perhaps easy to understand that there were significant exchanges of information in both directions during these early years. John Edye, Deputy to the Surveyor, Sir William Symonds, is reputed to have worked with Brunel in the design and build of the *Great Western*.

The first crossing of the Atlantic was by an auxiliary steamer, the *Savannah*, in 1819. Although something of a momentous event, she was actually on her way to be sold, rather than the start of a new service. She found no buyers and eventually re-crossed the Atlantic to serve out her days as a pure sailing ship, somewhat more profitably by all accounts.

It was not until 1833 that a full crossing under steam was to be attempted. In April of that year, HMS *Rhadamanthus*, crossed to the West Indies via Madeira and in August the *Royal William* crossed eastbound, oddly enough, once again an owner looking for a purchaser. In 1830 Britain had decided to send the mail to the Mediterranean by steam packet, a regular service that would be run by the Royal Navy until it was privatised in 1937. The forerunner of the P&O, the Peninsular Steam Company was formed in 1835 to run to the Spanish peninsula, but made little headway until it took over this mail service and the subsidy that went with it.

So by 1837 we have the start of regular steamship

---

1 A common usage still for merchant shipping.
2 The use of the word 'packet' to denote a ship is believed to have begun as early as the sixteenth century, when mail referred to as 'the packette' was carried on ships between England and Ireland.

services provided under the British flag, whilst the booming transatlantic trade remained in American hands.

IRON SHIPBUILDING

Iron boat building had already something of a pedigree by the time Brunel became convinced of its value for deep sea service and this was partly because of its superior carrying capacity and partly because of the shortage of good wood brought about by the demands of the Napoleonic Wars. The first vessel constructed by plate on frame was the *Vulcan*, conceived in 1816 for the Forth and Clyde Canal and launched in 1819. She set out the basics of riveted construction, plate on frame, that were to be followed in due course by the rest of the shipbuilding industry, and continued in service until 1873.

The first iron-built ship to provide a regular passenger service was the *Aaron Manby*, built in 1821 for the London–Paris through service. Again, as further confirmation of the strength of this material, it is of interest to note that she is reputed to have survived until 1880 before being broken up.

An early problem that had to be resolved before iron could be universally adopted was that of interference with the compass. As the amount of iron in wooden warships increased, so too did the problems with the compass. The Admiralty instructed the Astronomer Royal, Sir George Airy, to investigate the problem, building on earlier work by Captain E J Johnson in 1835. Airy succeeded in working out the basic mechanism for correcting a compass which is still used today, but it wasn't until somewhat later that enough experience had been gained to be sure of satisfactory accuracy every time.

Between 1819 and 1840s the iron foundries of Britain improved their capabilities to the point that sheet iron and sections were more readily available, although transport remained a problem, but by 1842 such was Britain's reputation for building iron ships that France sent their most eminent marine engineer and naval architect, M Dupuy du Lôme to report for his government on iron shipbuilding, a report that was published in Paris in 1844.

The years 1843 to 1845 were a significant period for our story, with many iron ships laid down. Included in this period were the big iron frigates including the *Birkenhead* and the *Simoom*. At 246ft (74.9m) excluding bowsprit, *Simoom* was considered one of the largest iron ships at the time of her building and, like the *Birkenhead*, was later converted to a troop ship, but she still came well short of *Great Britain's* 322ft (98m).

The famous 'tug-of-war' of 3 April 1845, showing the propeller-driven HMS *Rattler* (left) towing HMS *Alecto*, powered by paddle wheels, backwards at 2.8 knots. This was one of the last of a long series of trials involving *Rattler*, which had begun in October 1843, soon after completion at Sheerness dockyard, and which provided Brunel and the Admiralty with a mass of valuable data on screw propellers as a means of ship propulsion. The 'tug-of-war' was, however, a most graphic demonstration of the advantages of the new system. (© *National Maritime Museum, Greenwich, PY0923*)

3 | DESIGN AND BUILD

THE BENEFITS OF IRON CONSTRUCTION WOULD have been obvious to someone like Brunel, who certainly kept abreast of developments. Indeed, engineering development at this time was marked by a free exchange of information between people, mainly with little thought to personal advantage.

Brunel, then, was prepared to build the next vessel out of iron, despite the timber for the *Great Western*'s putative sister, the *City of New York*, having already been ordered. However, it would be several iterations of the design before that feature was finally incorporated into the studies in October 1838. The Rev Corlett in his book *The Iron Ship: The Story of Brunel's SS Great Britain* usefully allocated abbreviated titles, GB1 etc, to these various studies, with GB1 to 5 being all designed as paddle steamers.[3]

It is not until we get to GB6 (November 1840) that the screw propeller emerges as the selected means of propulsion. Overall, Brunel and his fellow members of the GWSC technical committee were occupied for at least two years completing the major design decisions, detail design going on well after that, of course.

As noted earlier, in addition to the visit of the screw-driven *Archimedes* to Bristol, it was during this time that Brunel became involved in the Admiralty's propeller studies and trials, leading to the building of HMS *Rattler*. There are a great many myths about the Admiralty and its attitude to technical advances, partly as a result of some off-the-cuff remarks made during this particular set of trials. The myth that the Royal Navy was against all advances, on the basis that they would render the existing fleet obsolete, probably has some small echo of truth in it, but in fact the Admiralty gave much support to many of the advances of the day, often safe in the knowledge that only Britain had the industrial might to put them into production in good time. However, myths are often more interesting than the truth, and this one persisted long enough to include *Turbinia* 'gatecrashing' a fleet review, when in fact the Admiralty had been funding Parson's research into steam turbines for some time before that.

Brunel was very much involved in the propeller trials and was given charge of the work by the Admiralty. The trials covered a wide range of propeller shapes and sizes and served to convince the authorities of the value of

the propeller over the paddle wheel. It is probably true that the result wasn't as clear cut as the propeller's proponents might have wished, hence the much-described towing match, *Rattler* against *Alecto*. Whilst this was good publicity for the propeller, an unbiased scrutiny of the facts would have shown that *Rattler* had much more horsepower at her disposal and would probably have won even if fitted with paddle wheels!

Brunel was probably already convinced, and had reported favourably to the technical committee on the feasibility of adopting the screw propeller, so proceeded to rework the *Great Britain* as a propeller-driven vessel. This had an immediate impact on the design of the engines, of course, and once more Brunel had his own ideas. A trunk engine had already been ordered from Humphreys and this had to be cancelled, an event that led to the resignation of Francis Humphreys and quite possibly to his early death shortly thereafter.

Brunel selected a variation of his father's patent triangle engine and it was resolved to build it in Bristol at the Great Western dockyard. As we have already noted, steam engines were by now reasonably well understood in the marine environment, but Brunel's decision to move to a screw propeller caused some layout problems. The reader will no doubt appreciate that the position of the drive shaft for paddle wheels is in completely the wrong place for a propeller. Having decided upon a variant of his father's patent triangle (or inverted V) engine it was a simple matter to arrange it so that the drive was aligned fore and aft along the length of the ship. Indeed, this in some ways fitted well within the chosen cross-section of the ship, with the cylinders resting on the solid foundations provided by the bottom structure at the turn of the bilge.

The drive remained well above the shaft, however. Added to this was the fact that the then current engines operated at a speed ideally suited to the rotation of a paddle wheel, whilst the rate of rotation required for a propeller was at least twice as great. A gearbox was obviously needed to solve both these problems, but Brunel's experience with the *Archimedes* convinced him that the noise of the gears would be unacceptable in a passenger ship, so he selected a form of belt drive. The belt was in fact several carefully designed chains arranged side by side, gearing up the engine speed by a ratio of 2.95 to 1 for the propeller shaft, and seems to have served its purpose well, as there do not appear to have been any recorded complaints about noise from passengers.

Brunel must have had considerable say in the design of the engine itself. The decision to cancel the

---

3 Ewan Corlett (1923–2005), engineer and naval architect, is regarded by many as the father of ship preservation in the UK. He generated huge support for the return of *Great Britain* from the Falklands, and was a leading light in her rescue and subsequent restoration.

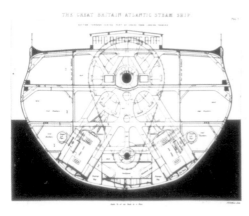

Left: Cross-section through the engine, by John Weale, nineteenth-century publisher of popular scientific works. The massive pistons, crankshafts and main drive wheel were a sensation in their day. *(The SS Great Britain Trust)*

Right: This medallion was struck as a souvenir of *Great Britain's* launch. *(The SS Great Britain Trust)*

Below: *Great Britain* was floated out of the dry dock, rather than 'launched', on 19 July 1843. Temporary masts and a funnel were installed for the sake of appearances, and she was later towed back into the dock for installation of the engines and final fitting out. *(© National Maritime Museum, Greenwich, PY8918)*

Humphrey engine included a resolution that the new engine would be built by the GWSC itself, and Brunel was the only team member with the necessary experience of steam engines. He specified four 88in (2.2m) diameter cylinders, a massive engine for its day and one which was effectively constructed as part of the ship's structure. The various supports and beams, being of considerable size and weight, were of necessity worked into the hull structure. It would be a number of years before engines could be hoisted in and out in a matter of hours or, at worst, days!

The necessary steam for the engine was supplied at a pressure of about 5 psi, by a seawater boiler. The boiler was effectively three separate boilers under a single casing, with furnaces at each end, totalling twenty-four, fed by coal from the surrounding bunkers.

The boiler used salt water which had been preheated

in a tank arranged around the base of the funnel. Using salt water was common at this time and brought with it its own problems, particularly the need to remove, or 'blow off' the concentrated brine that was produced once the water had been boiled off. In effect boilers of this period were just complicated mechanical salt pans! The *Great Britain* actually had a second system fitted which removed the brine continuously, adding its heat to the incoming boiler feed water. Whilst not the first use of feed water heaters, Trevithick's 1801 patent included a steam feed water heater: this must be one of the earliest marine applications.

Despite the considerable intellectual and industrial effort that had gone into it, this machinery arrangement was destined not to last very long. In fact it did not survive the disastrous stranding in Dundrum Bay (see page 19).

Whilst primarily a steamship, Brunel also provided a 'sail assist' rig designed to work simultaneously with the engines. This rig, as conceived, is an important and often overlooked part of the technology. It is an example of the engineer's mind being applied to the problems of making an efficient ship/machine. He decided on a rig of six masts fitted as a schooner, but with square sails on the main (second from the bow) mast. The whole was arranged to be operated from the deck by as few as ten to fifteen men, although all hands would probably have been turned out to set the square sails, the whole being a masterpiece in reducing labour, and hence crew numbers.

Conscious that it would be difficult to put masts through the machinery and shaft spaces, he devised a combination of deck hinge and iron wire stays for the after masts. He selected iron wire for its stability; it did not stretch as did natural fibres, which then required the stays to be continuously adjusted over time. Once set up, the deck hinge allowed the masts to be set within a small arc and permanently stayed in that position for the voyage, another labour-saving device.

A further problem had also presented itself during the design process; as the ship got bigger, so the size of the dock gates became a constraint. This has had a lasting effect in that the shape of the *Great Britain*'s midships section seen today is quite unique, and was arrived at as a shape that would permit the ship to exit Bristol's docks without damage. Had there been no such constraint, it is believed that the *Great Britain* would almost certainly have followed the simple shape of the *Great Western* and would now be seen as very modern indeed, anticipating the slab-sided ships with which we are now so familiar, instead of apparently harking back to the likes of HMS *Victory*.

She was launched in the presence of the Prince Consort on 19 July 1843 with typical Victorian panache, before a celebratory crowd of Bristolians, all anxious to see this new marvel of Brunel's.

LAYOUT OF THE SHIP

This then was the *Great Britain*; at 322ft (98m) the largest ship in the world at her launch. As designed for the transatlantic route she was fitted out for a total of 252 first- and second-class passengers.

The first-class accommodation was arranged on two decks from the stern to the machinery space, the second class from the forward end of the machinery space to the fo'c'sle, which itself was given over to the crew's accommodation.

Below the accommodation decks were the cargo holds. These were not designed for bulk cargoes, rather the carriage of high value packages and passengers' luggage, thus the access was 'discreet', to say the least. There were two decks below the second-class accommodation with a further pair of cargo lockers on each of the accommodation decks, whilst there was but one deck for cargo below the first-class accommodation. Below the after cargo space was the shaft alley and the fresh water tanks.

The coal bunkers were arranged around the machinery spaces and in the holds immediately fore and aft of them. Little is known of the arrangements of the decks above the machinery, but it is understood that there were more cabins, WCs and walkways through between passengers' accommodation.

This layout would not remain unchanged for long, but the various alterations will be dealt with in the following section.

Right: Not only the first photograph of the *Great Britain*, but also one of the very first photographs of the pioneer Henry Fox Talbot. Like Brunel, Fox Talbot was something of a polymath, interested in photography, archaeology and mathematics, as well as serving as MP for Chippenham for a number of years. (© *National Maritime Museum, Greenwich*)

Below: A 1:38 scale waterline model of *Great Britain* by Bassett-Lowke Ltd, depicting her in her original configuration, and as she is displayed today in Bristol. The hull and deck have a number of sections cut away so that some of the internal space is shown. (© *National Maritime Museum, Greenwich, L2719-001*)

4 | CAREER

ACROSS THE ATLANTIC

Designed for the Atlantic route, the *Great Britain* got off to a slow start. After sea trials, during which she proved her ability to withstand some unpleasant winter weather, the GWSC directors were apparently quite happy to spend time displaying their ship to royalty, the nobility and an admiring public, first on the Thames and then in Liverpool, so that her first paying voyage did not commence until 26 July 1845, two years after her naming and float-out in Bristol.

Liverpool had been chosen as the home port for the Atlantic trade in 1842, after some years of experience with *Great Western* operating out of the confines of the port of Bristol. Unable to go up the Avon when fully loaded, she had been loaded from barges and cutters in the stream at what is now Avonmouth, an action which still attracted the full harbour dues. Not only could the *Great Western* come alongside in Liverpool, but the dues were considerably less, a serious commercial consideration.

Her captain for this period was Lieutenant John Hosken, RN, previously the commander of the *Great Western* on which he managed sixty-four successful

Atlantic crossings. He was not to be so successful with the *Great Britain*, unfortunately for him, the GWSC and their ship.

The *Great Britain* arrived in New York after a crossing of 14 days 21 hours, a total distance of 3304 nautical miles and an average speed of 9.4 knots. Her return to Liverpool was on 30 August, arriving home on 13 September. The *Great Britain* completed one more round trip that year, during which she lost her foremast in a squall and found herself amongst the shoals of Nantucket, some 30 miles north of where she should have been. As a result of this her propeller was damaged and she was docked in New York to make it safe. However, it finally disintegrated on the voyage home.

On arriving in Liverpool she entered winter lay-up and maintenance. During this interval a new propeller was fitted and improvements made to the boilers, which much increased their steam generating abilities. Brunel's labour-saving rig was also altered, apparently in an attempt to better balance the rig to ease the amount of helm needed. The third mast was removed and the fourth became a twin of the mainmast. The

This fine engraving by the Bristol marine artist Joseph Walter depicts *Great Britain* under full sail, with topsails, all square sail and three jibs all set as she runs downwind. The full-rigged ship in the background serves well to demonstrate the new vessel's radical six-masted rig. (© *National Maritime Museum, Greenwich, PY8916*)

deck hinges were removed and the masts taken down to the 'tween decks, and the iron wire gave way to hemp for no clear reason it seems. Trysail masts were fitted to the two square-rigged masts with a gaff at their peak. This would allow the gaff to move up and down where they would otherwise foul the hoops on the two built-up masts.

During 1846 she successfully completed two more double crossings, but there were hints to show that Hosken's navigation was not what it used to be, as he again lost his bearings and scraped a reef off Newfoundland. Worse was to come. On her next voyage the *Great Britain* left Liverpool on 22 September 1846 at 11am. By 9.30pm she was firmly aground in Dundrum Bay; having failed to turn north once past the Isle of Man.

Much has been written about the reasons for her grounding, Brunel's involvement in the efforts to get her off, finally successful in August 1847, and the failure of the GWSC; suffice it to say here, that although surprisingly intact, the *Great Britain* had finished her career on the Atlantic and was about to enter on a new, longer, and very successful phase.

AUSTRALIA AND THE 1852 REFIT

The *Great Britain* was sold at auction to Gibbs, Bright and Company, one of whose interests was the Eagle Line, with sailing packets to Melbourne, Australia. The *Great Britain*'s forced sale had coincided with the discovery of gold in Australia. When this news reached Britain, there was such a rush to emigrate that the existing ships were overwhelmed. Adding the *Great Britain* to the route would add some much needed extra capacity.

To fit her for this service she was given an extensive refit, ranging from new engines to additional

Above: The final stages of the ship's rescue from Dundrum Bay. A trench was dug through the sand to help release her. The great boxes near her side had been filled with 50 tons of sand and, hung from pulleys, were intended to assist in lifting the ship so that the bottom could be repaired. Later, they were used as camels, or buoyancy tanks, when the tide rose. *(The SS Great Britain Trust)*

Left: A watercolour sketch of the weather deck during a Crimean trooping voyage. Judging by the stance of many of those present the ship was just departing from the UK and fond farewells were being exchanged. *(The SS Great Britain Trust)*

Below: The additional superstructure with extra accommodation can clearly be seen in this 1857 drawing of the longitudinal section or inboard profile of the ship, prepared for the Australian run. *(The SS Great Britain Trust)*

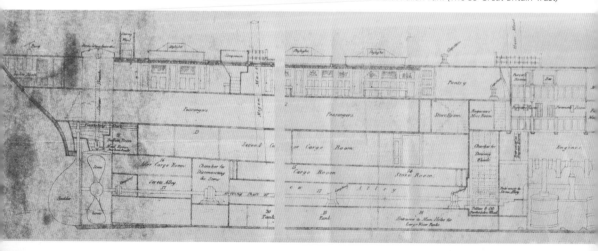

accommodation. As the original engines had been damaged at Dundrum Bay, these were replaced by a smaller arrangement, an in-line engine manufactured by John Penn and Company, consisting of two oscillating cylinders driving the shaft through an arrangement of gears. The boiler was replaced by two more advanced ones arranged side by side, fitted with steam-smothering connections, possibly the first time this fire-fighting system had been installed at sea.

Externally she gained side-by-side twin funnels and lost No 5 mast, all above an extra deckhouse that had been built on to increase the accommodation to 730, of which only fifty were first class. At the same time, cargo space was increased by stripping out the lower cabins and refitting the main deck accommodation solely as cabins, the saloons now being in the deckhouse.

After a shakedown trip to New York and back, she started on the Australian route on 21 August 1852, a service she was to continue with only a few interruptions for the next twenty-four years. The main interruptions, apart from a further refit in 1853, consisted of trooping duties, first to the Crimea during that war, and then once to Bombay during the Indian Mutiny.

The 1853 refit once again altered her sail plan. It would seem that at her previous refit her owners still had in view that steam power would be preponderant, whereas it was very much the auxiliary means of power on this route, and the first sail plan was by no means the best for long days of running before the wind from the Cape of Good Hope to Melbourne. So she became a three-masted clipper, to the casual viewer no different from any other vessel, except perhaps still for her size.

A further refit in 1857 was needed following her return from the Crimea. During this work her rig was changed yet again, and whilst remaining a ship rig it was of a much larger scale, more fitted to the size of the vessel and resulting in what was probably the biggest such rig ever. Her deckhouse was extended to become a proper superstructure, the boiler uptakes altered to exhaust through a single funnel, and a hoisting screw fitted to allow her to make full use of the new rig. Apart from another shakedown voyage to New York, she was back on the Australia route from 16 February 1857. This was followed by the trooping run to Bombay and then it was back to Australia until her final voyage of February 1876.

Her service as a passenger ship had come to a forced halt primarily as a result of Brunel being ahead of the field again. For insurance reasons her owners were anxious that their ship should be classed under the new system of rules that had developed since her launch, but Brunel's design did not fit into these rules, and despite the Lloyd's Surveyor noting her structural soundness, the committee that governed Lloyd's did not feel able to assign a class to her in view of this and also of her age.

SAILING SHIP DAYS

The *Great Britain* was left moored at Birkenhead and after a failed auction was taken in hand by her owners' latest incarnation, the Liverpool company having been taken over by its London counterpart, becoming Anthony Gibbs, Sons and Company. With their interests in South America, it seemed logical to strip out the passenger accommodation and the engines, and sail her as a pure sailing ship to the west coast of South and North America.

She retained the sailing rig of 1857, but lost her engines and passenger accommodation. In addition a wooden sheathing was bolted to the exterior of the hull. The true reason for this has been lost in the mists of time, various theories being put forward from

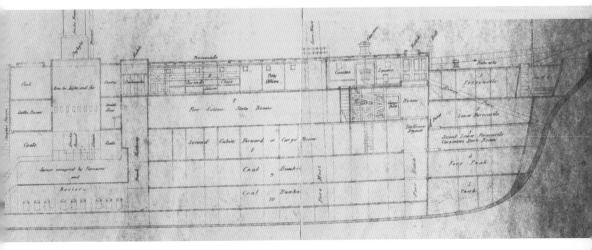

Left: Passengers shelter under a deck awning in 1874, during the Melbourne–Liverpool voyage which she completed in 64 days. *(The SS Great Britain Trust)*

Below: Riding to a mooring at Gravesend, 14 August 1875, just before sailing on her last voyage to Australia, with her three-masted ship rig and the sail-assist machinery. The accommodation ladder on her port side leads into the promenade deck. *(© National Maritime Museum, Greenwich, G01948)*

This and the next few photographs show the *Great Britain* in the Falklands. This first was taken shortly after her arrival although work has obviously started on turning her into a hulk, as all the top masts and rigging have already been sent down. *(The SS Great Britain Trust)*

fendering whilst loading from barges to protection against fouling. Whilst it was not uncommon to girdle a warship in this way to improve stability, the *Great Britain* had been if anything too stable, but it may be that her new owners did indeed feel that the removal of the machinery would have needed counteracting in this way. It was in this condition that she served out her last four years afloat sailing between Liverpool and

This shot could be earlier than the one above as work is clearly in progress, but the main yard seen rigged above is here lying on deck. There remains some running rigging still to be seen and the canvas covers would not have survived long after being hulked. *(The SS Great Britain Trust)*

San Francisco around the Horn, a route known to many 'Down Easters' from New England. Like many of these Down Easters her fate was to be decided by the sometimes extreme weather around Cape Horn.

In the *Great Britain*'s case, outward bound from Penarth with a cargo of coal in late April 1886, her master, Captain Henry Stap, tried for over thirty days to round the Horn against near-hurricane force winds. The decks were leaking, the cargo had shifted and fore and main topgallant masts had been lost, before the crew finally persuaded Captain Stap to turn back and seek shelter at Port Stanley in the Falkland Islands. Despite the appalling weather and the battering she had received, a subsequent survey showed her hull to be quite tight, but the local estimate for the repairs to her rigging was enough to have her written off as a constructive total loss.

HULKED

Although this marked the end of her active life, the *Great Britain* was about to embark on a fourth and final working career as a floating storehouse or hulk. Sold to the Falkland Islands Company on 8 November 1887, she was stripped down to her lower masts and doors cut into her side, and used as a wool and coal store.

For fifty years she remained at anchor off the Town Jetty of Port Stanley, visited from time to time by passing seamen who knew something of her history, until the time came to replace her with a newer and therefore less risky vessel. Although the subject of an early attempt at preservation she was finally moved to Sparrow Cove where she was scuttled. Here she remained until the next and final phase of her career opened up.

The *Great Britain* as a working store. Most of the rigging and spars and masts have been cleared away, the boats gone and the main yard re-rigged as derrick of sorts to load and unload as necessary. *(The SS Great Britain Trust)*

5 | RECOVERY

IN NOVEMBER 1967 THE LATE EWAN CORLETT wrote to *The Times* reminding everyone of the existence and importance of the *Great Britain* and suggesting 'at least' she be documented, 'at best' she be recovered and put on display.

In his own words (at the 1990 Society of Oxford University Engineers Dinner), 'When I first wrote to *The Times* suggesting that something should be done about THE GREAT BRITAIN – and got an overwhelming response – quite a few people, including I fear, my wife, thought I had gone mad. The ship was 8000 nautical miles away, virtually in the Antarctic, was a wreck and 123 years old at the time!' The 'overwhelming response' provided the important impetus· needed to set in motion a train of events that finally resulted in the vessel as we see her today. The letter produced some immediate responses from a body of 'seriously interested and energetic people', to quote the Rev Corlett again, who formed the SS *Great Britain* Project in May 1968. Various visits and inspections over the years by interested parties had produced a variety

of conflicting opinions on the state of the vessel and on sifting through these it rapidly became apparent that a professional survey would have to be carried out.

Taking advantage of the offer of a passage from Montevideo on the ice patrol ship HMS *Endurance*, Rev Corlett went out to Port Stanley in November 1968, and with much appreciated help from the Royal Navy completed the first proper engineering survey of the hulk. His description of the survey in *The Iron Ship* makes fascinating reading, and after assessing his findings he was able to conclude that the *Great Britain* was capable of salvage.

One area of concern which must be included in this narrative is the large crack that had developed from one of the doors which had been cut through the gunwale. This crack had opened up after her scuttling, as both the bow and stern were found to be unsupported where tidal scour had washed out the sand beneath them, and a hog had developed. Naturally there was concern that careless handling during any recovery

Many years later, the scene hasn't changed that much. The background is now Sparrow Cove instead of Stanley harbour and much of the deck fittings and woodwork have decayed, but the masts and the main yard remain. This shot was taken during the recovery survey, the one on the following page is just a bit before this one. *(The SS Great Britain Trust)*

Left: Sparrow Cove and a derelict *Great Britain* untouched for many years, but still with the main yard rigged. Notice the steady decay of the deckhouses. but not yet total as shown in the previous shot. *(The SS Great Britain Trust)*

Right: Another of the 1965 survey photographs looking this time toward the bows. The decayed deck planking is obvious here and presented a problem to the surveyors when the final detailed survey was carried out for the rescue mission. *(The SS Great Britain Trust)*

would cause irreparable damage, and so the crack would have to receive some extra attention, although Corlett felt that the crack would close up once the hog was taken out.

Armed with his findings, Ewan Corlett returned to the UK and reported back to the Project. Based on the report, they arranged for a towage company to look at the vessel with a view to making her watertight and then towing her back to the UK. Their report was not favourable, however; they considered that it would be quite impossible to tow her home, so a second approach was devised. This time the proposal was to put the vessel onto a barge and tow that home. A meeting was held with the eventual contractor in late December 1969 which was most positive.

So once again, the *Great Britain* was to be success-fully salvaged, this time during April 1970. Much credit must go to the quiet professionalism of the salvage company, but also to Ewan Corlett's assessment of the situation in which he found the ship. With the crack reinforced it behaved exactly as he had predicted and closed significantly once the *Great Britain* was placed on an even keel on the barge for her tow across the Atlantic, a rescue made possible by several large dona-tions, including ones from Sir Jack Hayward, and the late Sir Paul Getty.

In addition to Ewan Corlett's own record, much has been written about this episode and one of the real benefits of the internet was graphically illustrated by coming across filmed interviews of the people involved in the recovery operation during the research for this book.[4] In addition to the comments from the team, this particular reference also includes amateur film shot locally of the recovery process and the departure on the voyage back across the Atlantic,

---

4   http://www.nonesuchexpeditions.com/video/ss-great-britain/Plh_2010715149_2/ss-great-britain.htm

successfully carried out during the summer months.

It will be recalled that the size of the *Great Western* had encouraged the GWSC to move their operations to Liverpool, as the ship was unable to get into Bristol proper at loaded draft. The problem of access to Bristol was to be faced again with the recovered *Great Britain*. She was floated off the pontoon at Avonmouth and dry-docked for more reinforcing of that crack and then waited for a suitable lull in the weather for the tow up the Avon to Bristol and her future home, back in her building berth.

After a short wait and a passage up the Avon, arriving in Bristol's Cumberland basin on 5 July, she was docked on 19 July 1970 in the Great Western Dock, exactly 127 years after she had been floated up from the same dock, this time in the presence of HRH Prince Philip, nicely reflecting the presence of the Prince Consort at her naming.

Ewan Corlett, who had done so much to bring her home, wrote in his book, *The Iron Ship*, that,

one was reminded irresistibly of all that had happened since this great ship had last floated on this river. Virtually the whole history of iron ship-building, and all the history to date of steel ship-building and the screw propeller, had occurred since then; Britain had risen to absolute dominance as a shipbuilding nation ...; Victoria, the young queen who trod the decks of the ship in 1845, had grown old and died, and her great-great granddaughter now reigned; the Indian Mutiny, the Boer War and two World wars had changed Britain out of all recognition. In *Great Britain*'s youth even the rail-ways were young; the whole of modern technology developed since she left the Avon. With her help the great nation of Australia had grown up during her lifetime. No other British ship except the *Victory* had been so important to her country.

Above: *Great Britain* under tow, and on her own bottom, on a flooding tide on the Avon, 5 July 1970. **Below:** Passing under Brunel's Clifton suspension bridge which in 1844, when she'd first made her way down to the sea, was incomplete. *(The SS Great Britain Trust)*

6 | RESTORATION

MUCH HAS BEEN WRITTEN OVER THE INTER-
vening years on the best approach to the restoration of historic ships. Indeed, there are now government-sponsored guidelines available, running to many hundreds of pages of often hard-won experience, but in 1970 restorers were largely on their own. Several actions and decisions had been taken whilst the ship was on her way back, two of the most important being the decision to open to the public immediately, and also to appoint a project officer to oversee the yard and the ship during the restoration.

Joe Blake, Commander RN Retd, has written his own account of the next sixteen years but that only covers the first half of the story, restoration being an ongoing task.

The first requirement was to find out exactly what they had. It would be altogether too simplistic to view the ship as Brunel's. It had been altered and added to many times over the years and each change had left its mark. But to find these marks the hull had first to be cleared of mud and debris, a painstaking task done properly, but one which inevitably produces some interesting finds, in this case a complete original WC! Having removed the overlay, high-pressure water jetting was used to clean the structure back to bare metal, and arrest any ongoing corrosion. The bare metal was coated with red lead whilst still warm from the drying process. Externally, the wooden sheathing was removed and the bolt holes disguised with bolts that looked like rivet heads. The surviving structure could then be inspected and ascribed to one or other of the various phases of her career. It proved possible to identify much of the original structure, including, for example, the original stern frame, found under the 1857 additions.

When restoring a vessel, one of the first decisions called for by recent guidelines is that of the date to which she will be restored. In the *Great Britain*'s case a decision seems to have been made quite early to restore her externally to her 1844 state. This should not be taken as meaning anything not of this date has no value, of course, and modern guidelines are quite specific about conserving and recording all of the components of a vessel.

After cleaning and recording, almost as important was to make the hull and decks watertight. Not only because rain would undo the conservation of the iron almost as quickly as it was carried out, but also because the restorers expected to have to move within three years to accommodate the planned redevelopment of the area. However, despite some uncertainty about the permanence of the site, it was considered essential to restore the ship as much as possible as a visitor 'attraction' to keep a flow of income coming in. One of the most important aspects of this policy was the need for a replica engine and this was duly set in hand.

Much has already been written about the design, manufacture and installation of the replica machinery.[5] Although some original drawings had survived, the fragile nature of the ship dictated that much of the original wrought iron should be replaced by lighter materials, thus steel and aluminium alloy eventually found its way into the iron ship. But before the engine was to be completed, there were several events in the restoration process that had to be addressed.

By the 1990s several things had changed, not only with the *Great Britain* but also in the maritime heritage world in general. In 1979 the Australian International Council on Monuments and Sites published the Burra Charter, a document which formed the foundation for conservation best practice from then on. This was closely followed by the discovery and retrieval of the Royal Navy's first submarine, the *Holland 1*. Once recovered from the seabed she was treated for corrosion on the basis of best practice at the time and installed in the Royal Navy Submarine Museum at Gosport. It wasn't very long, however, before the museum became aware that the corrosion had restarted and this led to the discovery that the moisture from visitors alone was enough to reactivate chloride compound-based corrosion, and in 1993 plans were in hand to deal with this.

In the meantime the United States Department of the Interior had set up a variety of ways and means to preserve, conserve and restore US heritage. The most important from the maritime perspective were the so-called 'Green Book', the Secretary of the Interior's Standards for Historic Vessel Preservation Projects with Guidelines for Applying the Standards, prepared by the San Francisco Maritime National Historical Park and the National Maritime Initiative, in 1990, and the Guidelines for Recording Historic Ships, prepared by the Historic American Buildings Survey / Historic American Engineering Record (HABS/HAER), 1988. In 1992 the UK's National Historic Ships Committee was set up, leading eventually to the current National Historic Ships Unit and the National Register of Historic Ships (the *Great Britain* is 76 on the register).

---

5 See Joe Blake, *Restoring the Great Britain* (Radcliffe Press, 1989).

An event took place in 1994, at first not seen to be connected, but which was to have a major impact on ship restoration and preservation. The UK government had given the go-ahead for a national lottery, one of the major requirements of which was that the operator had to set aside a large part of the profit for good causes in Britain. Out of this came the Heritage Lottery Fund (HLF) as one of the organisations tasked with dispensing the money and, as things would prove, a major funder of heritage vessel preservation.

With arrival of the HLF several other pieces of the jigsaw fell into place. Based on the Burra Charter, the HLF required applicants to provide them with Conservation, Access and Audience Development plans as well as a business plan demonstrating a sustainable future for the applicant's project. Taken in conjunction with the Green Book, these documents were to form the backbone of maritime heritage restoration for the next few years.

At the same time the problems with the *Holland 1* were being worked out by its parent museum. The boat was immersed in a tank of sodium carbonate and an electric current passed between the structure and electrodes placed throughout. After almost four years of treatment the structure was found to be virtually free of chloride compounds, but to be on the safe side the boat is displayed in a humidity-controlled environment.

During the same period the *Great Britain* and her supporting teams underwent a few changes of their own. Various important figures retired and new people came in. As a direct result of the arrival of the HLF on the scene, there was a clear need to adopt a more rigorous approach to heritage artefacts, of which the *Great Britain* was probably one of the biggest. This was seen to dictate the need for museum curatorial experience, and after due process the *Great Britain*'s trustees appointed Matthew Tanner as their first professional curator.

Matthew came to the *Great Britain* when the need was to define a sustainable future for the vessel. Having been largely self-supporting since its arrival in Bristol, it had been very much a hand to mouth existence and as a result there were no reserve funds to cover major repairs or conservation work. It was also apparent that the early attempts at conservation were failing, much as those of *Holland 1*, and a new approach would be necessary.

The scale of the problem may be judged from the SS Great Britain Condition Report.[6] It clearly was a similar problem to that faced by the *Holland 1*'s owners, but equally clearly it would be difficult if not impossible to immerse the whole hull in electrolyte, and equally impossible for the organisation to survive for four or more years without income. However, it was considered practical to exercise control over the humidity of the environment around the vessel's hull. This has been achieved by the installation of an innovative false waterline, effectively a glass roof to the dock, plus the installation of a sophisticated air conditioning plant that supplies dry air to both sides of the iron hull. Whilst much research was being carried out at various institutions around the country, the Trust commissioned Cardiff University to carry out a study of the *Great Britain*, which concluded that so long as the humidity is kept below 22 per cent, the chloride-driven corrosion will be held in check. Thus the dock below the waterline has become an air-conditioned space to preserve Brunel's structure for the foreseeable future. The next problem was sustainability, and here the reader is referred to the Conservation Plan on the SS *Great Britain* website. For perhaps the first time, the whole site was being considered and being utilised for the benefit of sustaining the *Great Britain* into the future.

As a result of much hard work, mainly from the curator, but also from a variety of volunteers and consultants, this new vision was gathered together in a successful application to the HLF for funds. In addition, the team also had to raise their share of the necessary money towards an overall bill of £10 million.

The result is what today's visitor sees: the dock is now surrounded by restored or rebuilt buildings, including the new south range, which, whilst echoing very closely the original GWSC steamship engine factory, contains modern flats, the new Brunel Institute and a modern reception, visitor centre and shop for the *Great Britain* site. In additon to the new ticket office and reception area, the Brunel Institute includes conservation facilities; a library and archive containing thousands of books, plans, models, photographs, artworks, films and other material relating to Brunel, *Great Britain* and to the wider field of maritime history; a lecture theatre; seminar rooms; and other education and teaching facilities.[7]

---

7 http://www.brunelinstitute.org

Right: An aerial view of SS *Great Britian* sitting in her dry dock in the redeveloped Great Western Dockyard, just a small part of the wider ongoing redevelopment of Bristol's historic docks for residential and leisure purposes. In the background is the city centre and in the distance, at the very top of the photograph, can be seen Temple Meads railway station. *(Photograph: Commission Air)*

---

6 Available from the SS *Great Britain* website (see Bibliography).

THE HULL

A view of the iron hull that says as much about the durability of the material as it does the elements it has had to weather. The unmarked plates reveal where badly corroded originals have been replaced during restoration

THE EXTERIOR IS A NEAR PERFECT RESTORATION
of the vessel as she was when first floated out of this
dock in 1843. The iron construction offered a number
of significant advantages over traditional wood: greater
cargo capacity (thick timber frames were replaced by
thin iron ones), finer lines and thus greater speed, and
greater strength. Despite the modernity of her iron
construction, however, elements of tradition remain,
particularly in the decoration, or gingerbread, both
here at the stern and at the bow (see page 44). Hand
carved from timber such as oak or elm and then
covered in gold leaf, such decoration was still to be

found on Royal Navy warships up to the end of the
Victorian era, long after it had been abandoned by the
bulk of the merchant fleet.

Above: The coat of arms of the City of Bristol, which depicts a
ship leaving harbour, symbolic of a city built on maritime trade
including, until shortly before *Great Britain*'s launch, the
notorious three-cornered slave trade that saw Bristol become
the main entrepôt for tobacco. This crest was also chosen by
the GWSC as their coat of arms.

Top: The traditional stern gallery, here giving light to the
passengers' promenade saloon, not the captain's cabin as
might be supposed.

Bottom left: The cornucopias, a symbol of bounty or
fruitfulness, individually hand crafted and added to the side
galleries either side.

Opposite top: The windows in the quarter galleries are false,
or blind. Despite this, the originals were fitted with curved
glass over the iron plate. The restoration has replaced
expensive curved glass with steel sheet with little loss of
authenticity. Above the galleries is a gilded swan.

Opposite bottom: The square transom and, below it, the
elegant curved counter stern, lit from below.

A WALK AROUND THE CRAMPED DOCK GIVES A good impression of the size of the vessel, the scrupulous attention to detail of the restored figurehead and trailboards and the stern gallery, and the elegant simplicity of her six masts. This panorama clearly shows the layout of Brunel's original design, but the empty harbour beyond tells its own story as do the rows of new flats and offices where once stood busy wharfs and warehouses.

SS *GREAT BRITAIN*

Displacement	3,675 tons
Dimensions	Length 322 feet (98 metres) overall, beam 50 feet 6 inches (15.39 metres), draught 16 feet (4.9 metres).
Machinery	Twin-cylinder, 1,000hp, direct-drive steam engine, with three boilers.
Complement	130 officers and crew.

Far right: The replica lamp tender's hut. Note the barrel of whale oil (labelled sperm oil), a product fundamental to lighting and lubricating the world long before the production of coal gas or the refining of mineral oil. The demand for the commodity was such that over 800 whale ships could have been at sea during *Great Britain*'s first voyages.

Right: Scales for weighing luggage and cargo before loading. *Great Britain*'s holds were arranged for only comparatively small packages and small scales like this would have sufficed.

Right: *Great Britain* was built in the Great Western Dock, excavated from a smaller dock specially for her construction. Unusually, she was built with her bows facing towards the dock entrance, contrary to 'normal' practice. Docks were generally shaped for the ship's bow to be at the landward end, which saved some labour when digging out the dock, and also ensured that the bowsprit and any associated rigging was over dry land, not out over the water and vulnerable to passing traffic. In the case of the *Great Britain*, the dock is not at right angles to the harbour anyway and Brunel's positioning was probably encouraged by his need to build the biggest ship possible in the space available. Alongside is the replica of Cabot's *Matthew*, which in 1997 followed the same course as John Cabot in 1497. The photograph shows well the growth of ships in the intervening 400 or so years. *(Commission Air)*

Below: Barrels stored on the dockside as though awaiting loading for the next voyage. There is no longer any hint of the foundry nor any of the other facilities of a shipbuilding yard.

Bottom: A view down the starboard side of *Great Britain* gives a clear indication of the tight of the ship in her dock.

Looking forwards from the stern, one pair of crane davits for a ship's boat stand proud of the hull, and just forward of them are two brackets without the davits. *Great Britain* was painted in the typical manner of a mid-nineteenth-century merchant ships with a black hull and false gun ports painted on the sides, by then a longstanding tradition of merchant ships which wanted to give the impression that they were armed and could look after themselves.

In her confined dock, the length of freeboard running forwards is impressive and would have been even more so to her contemporaries, contemplating as they were the largest ship of her day.

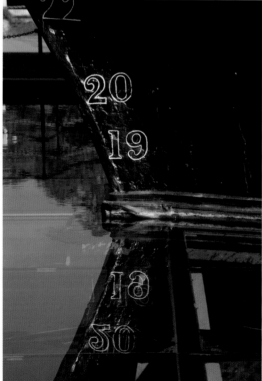

There are two sets of hawse pipes for the anchor cables. The lower set are Brunel's originals, whilst the upper set was added when she was converted for the Australian run in 1853. Her greater displacement meant that she settled lower in the water than originally planned.

Above: The two sets of hawse pipes are clearly visible in this photograph.

Opposite: The lower of the two sets, *Great Britain*'s original ones. Note the draught marks showing that she is apparently drawing 18 feet forward, which is 2 feet deeper than her design draught. This set was restored after she returned to Bristol and no sign of them can be seen on photographs of her lying at anchor in the Falklands.

Left and below: The shallow film of water around *Great Britain*'s waterline reflects the hull in the ever-changing light and weather and brings the ship to life.

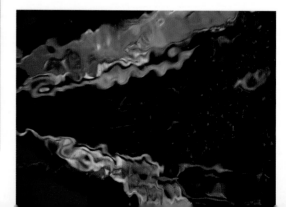

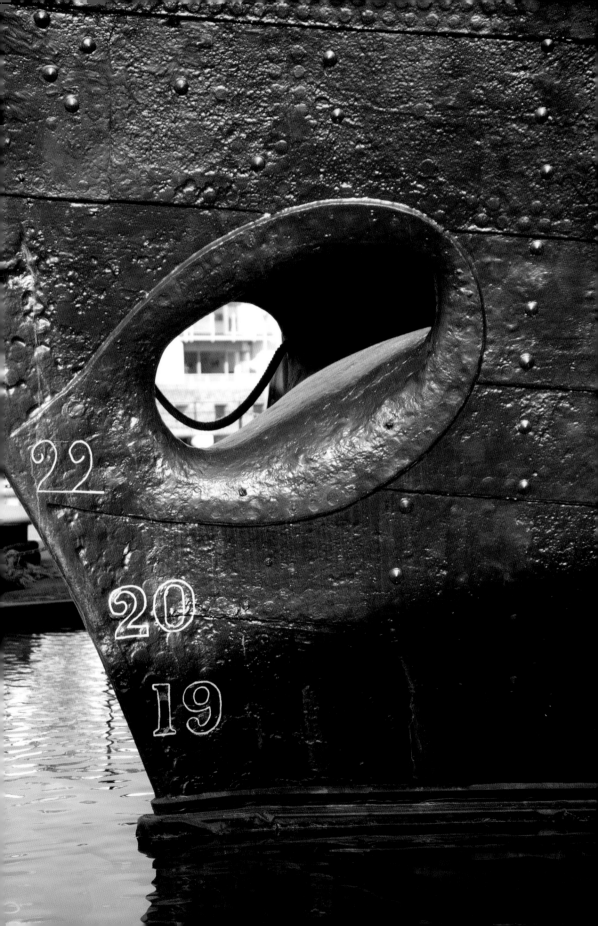

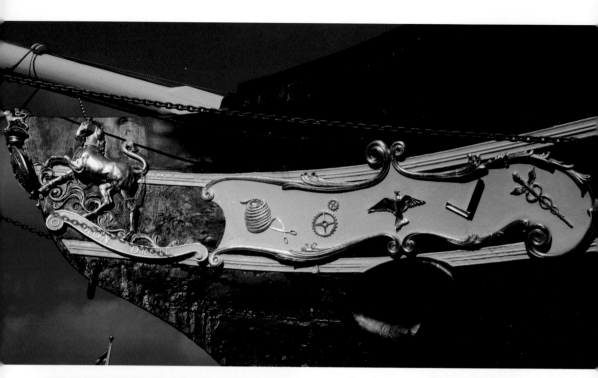

The bow of *Great Britain* incorporates decoration in the form of a figurehead and, just aft of that, the trailboards. All are based on hand-carved masters prepared by local sculptor Brian Rothnie who used the remains of the originals as guides. The originals would have been hand-carved from hardwood, usually oak or elm, but these replicas are in glass-reinforced plastic (GRP).

Top and above: Two views of the trailboards also showing the upper hawse pipes added after *Great Britain's* refit for the Australian service. The port side of the figurehead is a unicorn. The symbols on the trailboards, which differ from one side to the other, represent various arts and crafts. On the port side are a rope coil, gear wheels, a dove of peace, a carpenter's square and a wand; to starboard a bunch of flowers, a book, an artist's palette, trumpets and a lyre, a globe and a sheaf of corn.

Right: The lion on the starboard side of the figurehead.

Opposite: An unusual view of the figurehead from directly ahead, which also demonstrates the fineness of the cutwater, the part of the bow that cleaves the water as a vessel plunges into a sea. The figurehead is made up of the Royal Arms, flanked by the unicorn to port and lion to starboard.

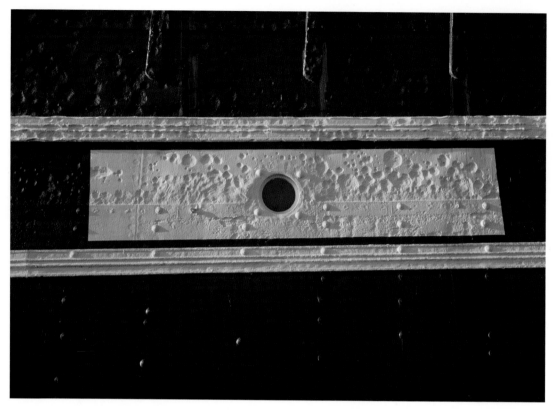

Above: The white painted band and imitation gunports are interrupted by portholes which illuminate the spaces on the promenade deck.

Below: The second row of portholes lit the saloon deck below.

Below: The uppermost strake of plating clearly reveals the marks left by the chain plates that were fitted when the masts were repositioned with changes to the rig. The present chain plates were fitted during restoration to her original six-masted configuration.

Opposite: A beautiful view along the ship's starboard side with the chain plates restored to their original positions. The old-fashioned tumblehome along the ship's side (the bulge and greater width above the waterline) was incorporated by Brunel to maximise the accommodation but at the same time allow the ship to pass through the nearby dock gates which only offered clearance of 44 feet near the waterline, narrower than *Great Britain*'s maximum beam higher up. This bulge would also have lessened the ship's rolling in a sea.

THE LIFEBOATS

Great Britain originally had six iron ship's boats, or lifeboats, which hung from crane davits. These boats were the subject of an 1843 patent and included flotation chambers to keep them afloat even if swamped. Four replicas, made of GRP, have been constructed for display and these can be seen on the dockside. Originally, three boats would have been hung from davits from each side.

Above: A careful examination of the boats reveals their closely-riveted structure. Displayed here on the dockside, turned up, the detail of the construction is much easier to see than if they had been hanging off the davits. Contemporary images indicate that they were hung so that the gunwale of the boat was level with the top of *Great Britain*'s guardrails.

Opposite top and middle: Weather covers keep out the rain. *(The SS Great Britain Trust)*

Opposite bottom: The National Maritime Museum model (see page 16) shows the six lifeboats in their davits.

A dry dock is traditionally closed by a gate or caisson. A gate can be hinged at its side or bottom, or run on rails sideways into a well. More usually a caisson is used and this is docked down and floated out very like the ships the dock is intended for. Once ballasted down with water it sits on a watertight seal and keeps the dock relatively dry.

Above and opposite top: The 1928 caisson in place. To ensure the dock is as watertight as possible another gate has been built outboard of this, rather than try and repair the caisson which would have meant taking it away just when it was most needed! Note the modern additions of supports for the glass roof.*(The SS Great Britain Trust)*

Left and far left: The wooden keel of the *Great Britain* sitting on wooden dock blocks. Wood is still used in many docks to this day as its ability to give a little will take up the uneven shape of a ship's bottom without the need to tailor each block. It should be understood that the bottom of a ship rarely stays as straight as when built, and resting unevenly on only a few blocks could introduce serious stresses into the fabric of the hull.

In the dock floor beneath the blocks can be seen the timbers inserted in order to stop the stonework moving under the load of a ship. Any movement of the dock bottom, however slight, could result in the blocks toppling and a ship falling into the dock.

The underwater hull is displayed beneath the glass roof and is probably the best place to get a good look at the plating of the vessel. The first iron ship of any consequential size, the *Great Britain's* plating is a reflection of the industrial capability of the time. This, as well as the means of delivery from forge to yard, dictated the size of plate available to the builder. There is clear evidence that the *Great Britain's* plate came from Coalbrookdale in Shropshire, in which case it would have been delivered by barge down the river Severn, although other sources suggest some came from the premier Low Moor Iron Works in Bradford, which could possibly have been used for repairs in Liverpool. At only 6ft (1.8m) long the *Great Britain's* plates were quite short and this has resulted in the many rivets to be seen along the hull. Later construction would feature 8ft (2.4m) plates which simplified the construction somewhat, whilst modern welded construction will use plates as long as 33ft (10m).

Left: The underwater hull below the glass roof of the dock. The plates above the keel are arranged so that they overlap the one above and are riveted together. This building method was very like the clinker planking of a wooden ship. Above this the plates overlapped the one below until about the sixteenth strake where the side became flush plated. Later vessels would have the plates arranged on an 'in and out' basis, that is, one plate would be overlapped top and bottom (the in plate) whereas the next plate would overlap top and bottom (the out plate). This arrangement lasted until the advent of welding.

The glass roof creates a giant dehumidification chamber and the pipes alongside the keel remove 80% of the humidity. This prevents corrosion caused by the chlorides – salt – trapped in the plates.

Right: Two views (from inside top and outside below) showing corrosion. By leaving them open the dry air can circulate and prevent further corrosion.

Below: Two close ups of the plates showing the overlapping plates and rivet heads.

Looking aft down the port side towards the propeller and the head of the dock. The original stonework and riveted hull are as one with the period of her build, but the necessary roofing supports and ventilation ducts are very much twenty-first century.

The rudder and six-bladed propeller are replicas, matching the original 'at launch' design. To save straining the 165-year-old structure these are both made of GRP, although the replica propeller itself was made by one of the most famous surviving British propeller manufacturers; Stone Manganese (now Stone Marine Propulsion), who started making propellers in the nineteenth century. The stern frame arrangement allows the balanced rudder to be hung well astern of the propeller. To ease the force required to turn a rudder blade, a portion of the blade is ahead of the pivot point and so that the water flow helps to 'push' the rudder over when it bears on this portion of the blade; it required careful handling under sail as it tended to fly over if the wheel was released.

Left: The palms of the propeller, attached to the arms, provided the main driving force, and tank tests have shown that the propeller would have been able to drive the ship at 12 knots though the pressure on the blades would have been considerable, about 2½ tons per blade.

THE LIFTING PROPELLER

Very much part of the vessel's heritage, the remains of her Australian rebuild have been conserved and are kept in the museum alongside the ship. Here we see the lifting frame and associated rudder which survived the ship's sojourn in Sparrow Cove.

The lifting frame was used to hoist the propeller clear of the flow when proceeding under sail and reduce the drag on the ship; this was a common feature of many ships at the later period of *Great Britain*'s life, and two other vessels survive in British museums with this feature, HMS *Warrior* at Portsmouth and HMS *Gannet* at Chatham.

Opposite: A replica of the massive lifting two-bladed propeller. The original propeller was the largest forging ever made of its sort. The tackle used for lifting the gear can be seen at the top of the frame. The blades were kept vertical when idle so that the water flowed past relatively unimpeded.

Right: A view of the rudder recovered with the ship. Note that with this arrangement of stern post, propeller and rudder it is not possible to retain a balanced rudder.

Below right: The other end of the lifting frame, inside the promenade deck. The trunk for the lifting frame passed through here to allow the frame to be pulled up from the weather deck.

Below: This photograph clearly shows how the frame with the propeller was hoisted up.

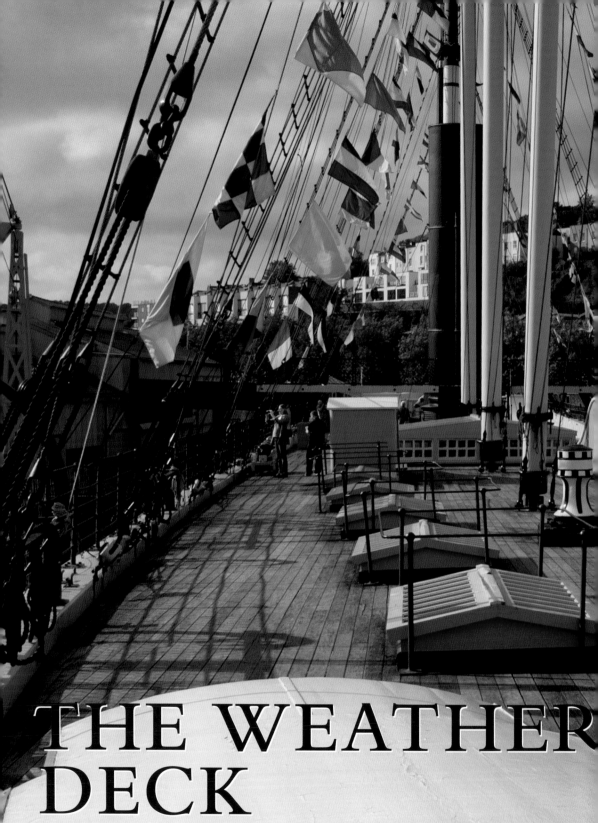

THE WEATHER DECK

The weather deck was the working deck of a sailing ship, but with the advent of
steam the space became used increasingly for the well-being of the passengers;
here are skylights to light the passenger accommodation, and space for exercise.

Though not fully rigged, a striking feature of the main deck is the apparent simplicity of the rig. Gone are the festoons of rope associated with a square-rigged ship such as the *Cutty Sark* or HMS *Victory*. Much of what meets the eye on this deck is for the benefit of the fare-paying passenger such as the skylights and companionways to the passenger accommodation. In addition, in the foreground, is the large skylight for the engine room.

Above: The ship's wheel with gratings for the helmsmen in place at its base, and the compass binnacle.

Centre: Evidence of the rigid segregation practised in passenger ships.

Right: The compass binnacle immediately in front of the wheel. This would be lit at night.

Opposite: Looking aft from the navigating bridge with the dominant teak engine-room skylight in the foreground. The great sweep of the wooden deck, no longer washed with salt water, is inevitably prone to rot. The most recent deck is steel backed, with an air gap between the wooden deck planks and the steel. There is little camber (curve) across this great deck, but what there is helps sustain the planking by keeping it free of standing water.

Opposite: The view forwards from the wheel. The captain's stage, or navigating bridge, is well forward of the wheel, just aft of the funnel. The large circular skylight in the foreground lights the promenade deck.

Above: Looking forward to the base of the mainmast, showing the position of the anchor windlass just forward of it. On the port side of the windlass is a warping drum, and in the distance the chain stoppers.

Right: A traditional hand-driven capstan, aft of the mainmast, which would have been used for sail handling.

Below: Merchant ships still carried cannon at this date, but these were only used as saluting guns or for attracting attention in an emergency.

The funnel and the navigating bridge are positioned amidships on the weather deck. The bridge is supported by stanchions and also fixed to the funnel superstructure. This bridge was probably only used when docking, when the Captain needed a better view than from far aft. The word 'bridge', however, has stuck to the navigating position of possibly every ship to date.

Opposite: The funnel seen from the bow. The Captain's stage, or bridge, behind it can be seen projecting on either side, while the dairy cow's pen is immediately in front.

Above right: Brunel had placed a feed water heater in the base of the funnel to heat the water going into the boilers. This area also contained the access to the engine room from the weather deck.

Above centre: The ship's one funnel with the Captain's bridge at its foot. The large pipe at the aft side of the funnel is for waste steam released from safety valves.

Left: The starboard end of the navigating bridge that extended to the ship's sides.

The equipment for working *Great Britain*'s anchors and cable was all arranged at the forward end of the weather deck and can be seen here. Forward of the windlass would have been kept a 30ft wooden ship's boat that could be swung out using the main yard as a derrick.

Below: The anchor windlass, which was driven by a unique specimen of a pump handle machine, worked like an early fire pump with two long handles attached at either end of the bar seen in the top left of the picture. This would have allowed ten to twelve men each side to raise the anchor.

Right: The port cathead. The anchors would be 'catted', that is secured, from the cathead when the ship was at sea. It is decorated with a lion's head.

Above: One of the main anchors stowed on the weather deck. Usually, this would have been hung off the cathead and made fast to the bulwarks during passage. This latter practice was known as 'fishing' the anchor. The anchor would have been released from the fishing to hang below the cathead when ready to be dropped.

Left: The cable lifter on the windlass, with a length of chain cable in place to demonstrate how it was gripped by the windlass.

Below: Detail of one of the anchors, which are replicas, made from resin.

Above: The ship's bell. One of the ship's original bells survived but this is a bronze replica, and it is mounted in an ornate replica 'dolphin' tabernacle, and situated in its original position, just aft of the forecastle. The bell was used at sea to mark the passing of time on board, time being measured in 'bells', for example eight bells would mark the end of a four hour watch at 4, 8 or 12 o'clock.

Above right: The cable clamps, known as chain stoppers. There is one for each cable and these were used to lock the cable once the anchor had been lowered, and remove the strain off the windlass, before the crew added a short length of cable to take the load to a deck fixture.

Top: The ship's dairy, just forward of the funnel. Here is situated the pen for the milking cows during passages. During her service on the Australia run the upper deck of *Great Britain* often resembled a farmyard, with sheep, pigs, bullocks, hens, ducks, geese, turkeys and rabbits, the majority being to provide fresh meat for the passengers. All of these in turn required tons of fodder, to be stored wherever possible.

Above: The manufacturer's plate on the top of the capstan. Clarke Chapman was formed in 1864, so this piece of equipment must have been installed as a replacement for a previous item. Clarke Chapman is still trading, but no longer lists capstans amongst their products.

Left: One of the outlets for the ship's bilge pumps.

MASTS & RIGGING

From the original six-masted rig, with several unique
features, through to the final sailing ship rig, thought to
be the largest ever fitted to a ship, *Great Britain*'s masts
and rigging were as novel as the rest of the vessel.

BRUNEL'S SIX-MASTED SCHOONER RIG WAS A masterpiece of engineering design and included such novel features as lightweight iron wire rope, and hinges at the feet of the four aft masts. The masts did not, therefore, have to be stepped through the decks where machinery and accommodation was located below.

The iron wire, which did not stretch, required none of the constant attention that hemp rigging needed as it stretched during a voyage. This helped keep the crew numbers down, as did the choice of fore-and-aft schooner rig, where everything could be handled from the deck, except the square sails on the mainmast.

The mainmast was the second mast from forward and the biggest. The iron hoops signify that it is a built-up spar made up from separate pieces, all bound together by the hoops.

Above: The mainmast with topmast above. Two square sails were set, the lower, larger one on a yard attached to the mainmast with a topsail above, on the topmast. The yards are no longer carried.

Above right: Five shrouds support the mainmast.

Right: Another of Brunel's innovations was to use iron bars, instead of bulkier hemp, for the ratlines in the shrouds. This was not only cheaper, but the reduced size also decreased windage. Hemp was re-introduced early in the ship's career.

Above: The hinge at the foot of No 5 mast. The two forestays visible here are those from mast No 6. In another engineering solution unique to the ship, the upward force of the stays counteracts the downward load of the mast to minimise the strain on the deck structure.

Left: A belaying pin at the base of the mast. Another characteristic was the lack of the various fife rails or bitts associated with sailing vessels of this era, as the simple schooner rig required far fewer halyards, sheets and other lines.

Below and opposite lower left and right: Chain plates with the shrouds attached. The rail behind is a pinrail to which sheets and other lines were made fast. The foremast is supported by four shrouds each side, and masts Nos 3 to 6 with just three shrouds a side, and the mainmast with five.

Opposite top: The base of the mainmast, stepped through the deck, looking forwards.

Left and bottom left: The lower ends of the two forestays for mast No 3 that are fixed to a mast band on the heavy No 2 mast, rather than to its base.

Above: Hempen rope coiled on the pinrail.

Above right: An upper deadeye through which lanyards are threaded so that the shrouds can be tightened up.

Right and bottom right: Single and double blocks can be found around the ship.

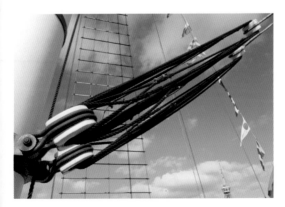

THE DEVELOPMENT OF

Great Britain carried a number of rigs during her long career, each designed to improve her performance, or fit better with the machinery. She was originally rigged as a six-masted schooner, and that is how she is displayed today, just as she was launched. Neither at her launch, or today, are the square yards or the gaffs for the fore-and-aft gaff sails in place.

Below and far right: The mizzen mast recovered with the ship from Sparrow Cove.

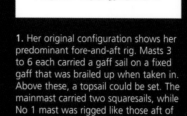

1. Her original configuration shows her predominant fore-and-aft rig. Masts 3 to 6 each carried a gaff sail on a fixed gaff that was brailed up when taken in. Above these, a topsail could be set. The mainmast carried two squaresails, while No 1 mast was rigged like those aft of the funnel. Three foresails could be set, two from the bowsprit.

2. During the first refit, in 1846, a number of alterations were made to the rig, probably to reduce the weather helm. The mast behind the funnel was removed and mast No 4 (now becoming the third) was increased in size and rigged like the original mainmast with squaresails, though a topgallant was added to both. These masts were also given trysail masts behind so that a spanker gaff sail could be raised and lowered without fouling the iron mast bands.

THE RIG

3. In 1852, No 5 mast was removed, so that only Nos 1 and 6 were left as originally designed. The gaff sails were given booms (the originals had been loose-footed), and these alterations were intended to improve performance both on and off the wind.

4. In 1857 she was completely re-rigged with a heavy three-masted ship rig and the big lower masts remained in her for the rest of her life, only being finally removed in Sparrow Cove in 1970. This was an enormous rig of 33,000 square feet (Brunel's original had been 16,000 square feet), and each of the massive lower masts was made from four trees, hooped with hinged iron bands.

5. In 1882 *Great Britain* was rebuilt as a sailing vessel. The engine machinery was removed, and the mainmast was moved forwards to better balance the rig which was now possible with the removal of the funnel.

Bottom right: The original main yard rigged on a mock up of the mainmast as it would have appeared during her days as a sailing ship. This was the yard that survived the ship's hulking in Port Stanley and was still hanging from its mast at the time of the rescue from Sparrow Cove.

Above: Looking along the top of the bowsprit. The two sets of deadeyes and lanyards seen here are for the fore topmast stays which lead along the bowsprit and then through blocks. The two chains are the lower end of the foremast fore stays, reflecting again Brunel's use of iron wherever possible.

Top right: The cathead used for stowing the anchors.

Right: The jack staff at the end of the bowsprit. The familiar Union Flag is only referred to as the Union Jack in this position.

Opposite, lower far right: The block and iron hanger attaching the bowsprit shrouds to the hull.

Opposite, upper far right: The chain in the centre is the bobstay, which holds the bowsprit down against the upward force of the foresails. The chains on either side are the bowsprit shrouds.

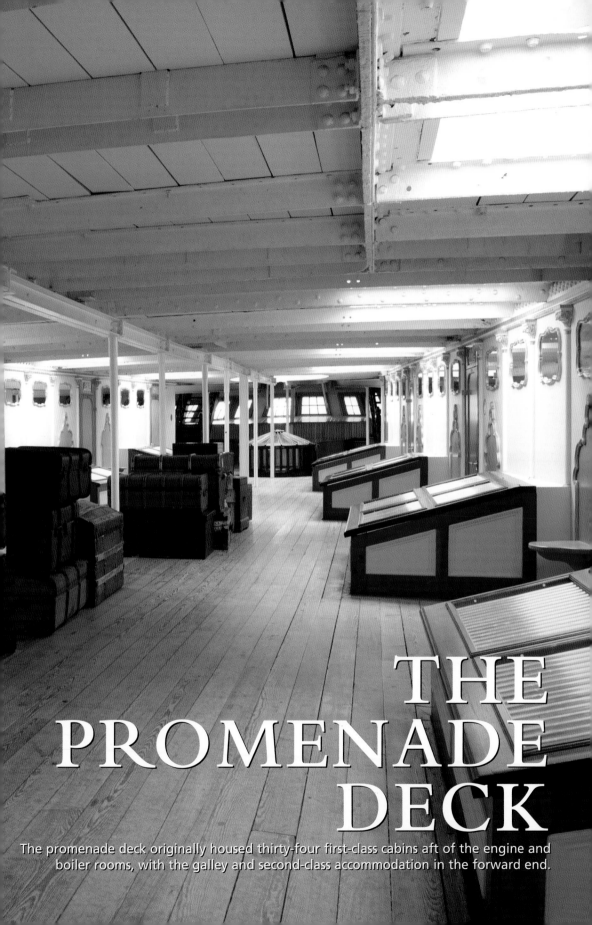

THE PROMENADE DECK

The promenade deck originally housed thirty-four first-class cabins aft of the engine and boiler rooms, with the galley and second-class accommodation in the forward end.

THE PROMENADE SALOON WAS ONE OF THE
Great Britain's architectural gems and has been
beautifully restored to near-original condition. The
intended clientele were used to staying in the best
hotels and would have expected nothing less of their
ship, and to this end the GWSC hired one of the best
London interior designers, the Crace brothers, to
produce a space that rivalled any hotel.

The area is lit by skylights along its length, as well as
by the stern gallery windows. At the stern, the prome-
nade saloon would have had companionways leading
both up and down, but the later insertion of the lifting
propeller resulted in the replacement of the down

companionway by the lifting trunk. Removal of this
during the original restoration was not considered to
be an option in view of the damage it might have done
to both trunk and hull and so it was covered by a
replica of the original round skylight. Stairs are also
located at the forward end leading both up to the
weather deck and down to the dining saloon

Either side of the promenade itself are the cabins for
the first-class passengers. The cabins are divided into
blocks of four, and reached via narrow transverse
passages. Between the doors into these passages are
located skylights that form light wells for the dining
saloon below.

Above: Looking forward on the restored first-class deck; a similar one would have been provided for second-class passengers further forward but this has not been replicated in the ship's restoration.

Above, right: A closer view of one of the skylights providing natural light to the dining saloon below. Note the open door into one of the side passages, the entrance to one of the groups of four first-class cabins. The many mirrors were intended to give the feel of light and space.

Right: Details of some of the decorative features on this deck, including a gilded royal coat of arms. The carvings in the restored interior were from the same local artist as the gingerbread and figurehead on the hull, Brian Rothnie.

Above: The aft end of the promenade deck showing the stern gallery windows to the right. It is also clear that the side galleries to be seen on the outside of the hull really are dummies for there are no signs of them behind Brunel's head where they would be expected. Out of shot behind the wooden bench on the right is the tiller head and steering gear that was exposed to the view of the passengers in the ship as she was originally built.

Right: A seat placed outside the passage, or lobby entrances, a place for the night steward to await his next duty or for the passenger to contemplate his or her surroundings, or recover from a twinge of seasickness.

Below, right: A typical cabin door plate.

Below, left: The joint of the weather deck to the ship's side. Note how the frame is carried round to line up with the deck beam, making for a very strong connection.

Above: An unusual view of the round skylight set in the weather deck. A second round skylight is in the deck immediately below, as shown in the photograph to the right. Originally, this skylight would have allowed natural light into the dining saloon below, but now it disguises the remains of the propeller-hoisting trunk.

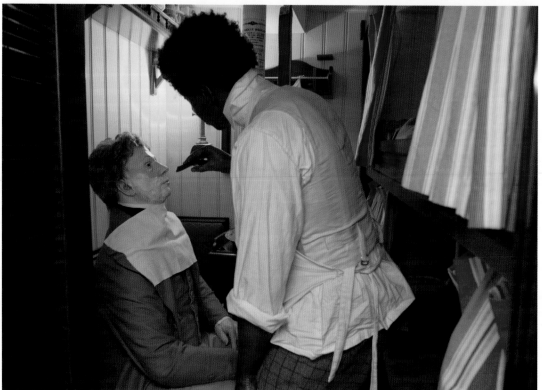

Opposite top: The purpose-designed surgery, depicting here an incident from 1860 when the surgeon, Samuel Archer, was trying to save an injured seaman's hand.

Opposite below: A feature of passenger ships was the presence of itinerant tradesmen who would set up shop in the cabins either at the request of the management or at least

with the approval of the Captain. Here a barber is at work.

Above: A typical double-berth cabin. Both first- and second-class cabins were small and cramped. Lighting would have been either oil lamp or candle and would have been tightly controlled by the crew to prevent fire, an ever-present danger on a ship at this time.

A large family cabin. The scene here shows Georgiana Bright, a passenger on *Great Britain*'s final voyage to Australia, in 1875. She is looking after her four young children, her unreliable governess having been dismissed and her maid being unwell. Meanwhile, her nephew is dying of typhoid fever in another cabin. Note the curve of the ship's side inwards towards the deckhead above. This panelling is placed inside Brunel's design of the structure joining the weather deck to the ship's side where the side frames are bent over to give a very strong structural connection, an expensive feature which rapidly gave way to a simpler joint in later ships.

Opposite: Another view of a double-berth cabin. The rifle appears to be a Henry rather than the better-known Winchester as it lacks the wooden 'forearm' of the Winchester. Both only came into use after the ship had been in service for many years, the Henry dating from 1860 and the Winchester from 1866.

Above: The reconstructed Ladies' Boudoir, off the main promenade deck. There would have been two of these originally with a toilet and stewardesses' cabins within easy reach. Voyage diaries tell us that gentlemen were sometimes invited in.

Left: One of the stewardess's cabins, and this poor stewardess is still to find her sea legs. Quarantine notices, like the one shown here on the right, were intended to reduce the spread of disease and illnesses onboard which could spread quickly throughout the confined space of a ship at sea, and would then require the ship to sit offshore until the appropriate quarantine period was up. This happened to *Great Britain* in 1854, during her third voyage to Australia, when smallpox broke out onboard and one of the crew died. A yellow flag 'Q' was hoisted to indicate this, and the ship had to spend nearly three weeks in isolation, watched over by HMS *Phantom*, an 18-gun sloop.

GREAT
BRITAIN

Steam   Ship

Notice of
QUARANTINE!

No person is to enter
THIS CABIN
other than with permission
of the DOCTOR

Charles Chapman, Commander

THE GALLEY

The galley has been restored to a configuration which the ship might have had during her Australian voyages, though then it would have been a deck higher, in the deckhouse that was built to house extra accommodation for the Australian emigrant trade. Little is known about this or the earlier galley, and the reconstruction is based on what is known about the galleys of contemporary sailing vessels and early steamships. Extensive research was carried out and a food historian brought in to advise on the food that might have been eaten and the equipment needed for preparing it. This small space produced meals for more than 600 passengers and crew, and was staffed by ten cooks.

Above: The small stoves, set against the forward bulkhead, were used for boiling and grilling. Above the stoves are shelves for keeping all the ready-use ingredients needed for the cooking. There was a dry food store onboard as well as a wet meat store, and only the food needed immediately was kept in the galley.

Left: The ready use store of ladles. Many of the utensils on display are Victorian, though not from *Great Britain* herself, and were acquired when the galley was reconstructed.

Above: Another view of the cooking range from across the preparation table in the centre of the galley.

Right: The central range. This was the main cooking apparatus and used for baking and spit roasting, though here the spits are stowed neatly away. They would have been fitted to the two brackets on the front of this stove and regularly turned. The heat coming from the top of the stove wouldn't have been wasted and large pans have been placed here in the restoration.

Dinner was relatively early, at around 6pm, and breakfast served around 8am, and between these times the fires would have been extinguished.

Opposite top: On each side of the galley are sinks. Here, on the port side, the restoration depicts the passengers' plates and cutlery waiting to be washed up. On a steamship the one thing in ready supply was hot water, so even if the ranges were not alight it would would still be possible to wash up.

Above: A closer view of the storage shelves above and behind the main cooking range. Look out for the rat scurrying along at the back of the shelves.

Left: We know that the Victorians liked their puddings, and the first-class menus confirm that jelly was served. Here is a selection of mostly Victorian jelly moulds and reconstructions of the finished desserts.

Left and below: The cook at the starboard side sink, beside the smaller cooking stoves, gutting fish. This area is depicted as the main food preparation area with the table behind him storing food in boxes and bins underneath.

Bottom: A good view of the range of smaller cooking stoves. Coal is shown stored beneath the fire doors. This would not have been the same coal used for the main engine, and it would have probably been stored somewhere in the cargo hold. The ingenious adjustable racks allowed the chef to vary the heat on the pots above the open coals.

Above: The bakery. Fresh bread would have been baked each day. The dough preparation area can be seen to the left, the two main ovens are in the centre, and the cooked bread racked to cool on the right. The barrel of flour is stowed next to the ovens to ensure it stayed dry. The paddles for placing the dough into the ovens and removing the hot bread are on the left.

Below left: The archway leading into the bakery, and the adjacent bulkhead, replicate the originals but are constructed with resin.

Below right: In this view we can see the small additional bake oven to the right. Adjacent to it are the cooling racks with fresh bread awaiting the next meal.

Left, top and bottom: These cabins on the starboard side, beside the engine room, were for the crew: not the seamen, but the purser, first and second mates, and engineers. The seamen would have been housed in the fo'c's'le. The stuffed seabirds were souvenirs, and there is reference to them in diaries, as there is to the monkey to be found in another cabin. Similar cabins to these, which can be found on the port side, again beside the engine room, were for second-class passengers.

Below: A washroom that would have been shared between the crew and the second-class passengers. Only the first-class passengers would have had access to bathrooms.

Above: The steerage and third-class pantries , or messes, with the food allowances of salt, sugar and jam set out for each group or mess. The emigrants in steerage would have been expected to fend for themselves in many respects and here we see the basic commodities and plates as supplied by the ship. They could prepare cold food, but hot meals were collected from the main galley and then served out here.

Right: One mess's rack of rations, platters and cutlery. The rations of staples, like sugar and ship's biscuits, were distributed each week by the ship.

Below: The ship's official registered number 'carved' on one of the iron main deck beams. This particular beam was once part of the frame of the central cargo hatch but has been repositioned during restoration, and is now at the after end of the steerage pantry.

As no drawings have survived from the period of *Great Britain*'s final refit for the Australian run, the exact layout and positions of the steerage and third-class cabins and messes must be conjecture. For the reconstruction of the ship they have been rearranged on the promenade deck where originally the second-class passengers would have had their facilities. During her time in the Australian emigrant trade, steerage accommodation was located a deck further down. However, a sketch in the diary of a passenger gives a reasonable indication of the layout, and that is what the present reconstruction is based on.

Below and opposite: The steerage and third-class 'dining saloon', or more accurately mess deck. The word mess originally comes, like many nautical terms, from a French word 'mes' meaning a portion of food or a serving. The tables are located on the outside of the ship to benefit from the natural light; when not needed they could be folded up. It was on these that all the meals in this part of the ship were eaten.

The cabins and sleeping areas in this part of the ship have been divided into third-class and steerage. The third-class cabins each contain four narrow bunks, and these might well have been taken by families. The steerage accommodation was along the sides of the transverse passages. Even these cramped conditions were better than those found on many contemporary emigrant ships, particularly those voyaging to North America, and *Great Britain* had a good reputation. The figures all represent real people and are based on diaries and journals.

Above: A passenger has just given birth and an older woman, acting as a midwife to the young passenger, holds the baby.

Right: A typical steerage cabin, arranged for four bunks, two of which can be seen here. The gentleman doing a little sewing is based on a passenger who has left a record of his voyage out to Australia where he was intending to work in the gold fields.

Opposite: A general view of the steerage accommodation, with its distinct lack of privacy. Trunks and cases are stowed under the bunks and clothing hangs from extemporised washing lines. Despite the length of voyages, pets were often brought along, and in the case of cats were useful for catching rats, an inevitable and unwelcome part of shipboard life.

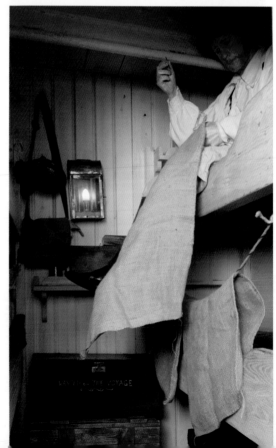

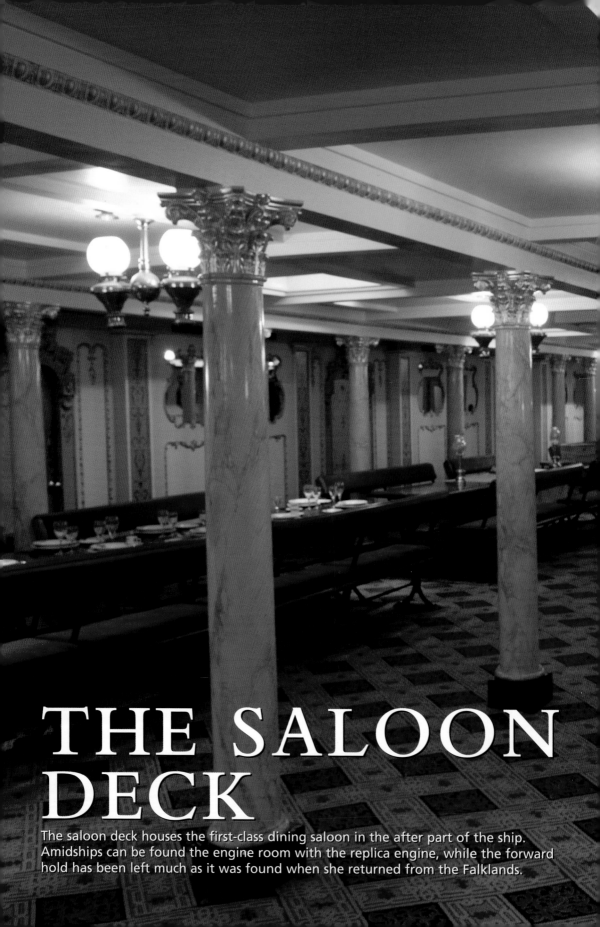

THE SALOON DECK

The saloon deck houses the first-class dining saloon in the after part of the ship. Amidships can be found the engine room with the replica engine, while the forward hold has been left much as it was found when she returned from the Falklands.

The first-class dining saloon is the second gem that has been restored to its original glory, though using modern materials. Lit by the light wells from the promenade deck above, the saloon features the two rows of tables from the original that are clearly depicted in contemporary etchings found in *The Illustrated London News*. Cabins for the first-class passengers were off this space. Now, on the port side is the modern kitchen for dining events held on the ship.

Above: The aft bulkhead of the dining saloon, with doors that would have led to cabins, and the mirrors that add light and a sense of spaciousness. The ornate decoration reflects the decor of the era and the very best hotels of the day, and the carpet is an exact reproduction of the original.

Opposite, top: The Corinthian columns at the sides of the saloon, all of them lightweight replicas. Contemporary newspaper reports indicate that the original columns were marble. The centre line of columns disguise metal strengthening supports.

Centre, right: The reversible seat backs shown in their two positions, The backs could be folded to face the table or, in this case, outwards as if for an entertainment in the centre of the saloon. The saloon was also a place to socialise as well as eat and the seat design would have encouraged this.

Right: The table set for dinner. The china service is an exact replica of the original, copied from a few remaining examples which were discovered.

The dining saloon, with its gilded decoration, is a fine example of Victorian style and taste, a style that the first-class passengers would have recognised and been familiar with from the grand hotels of this era. It was fitted out, as were other parts of the ship, by Jackson and Feen to the designs of the Crace brothers who had decorated Brighton Pavilion for the Prince Regent a decade earlier.

Top left: Once again the handiwork of Brian Rothnie is to be seen in the beautifully reconstructed pilasters and other decorations here on the aft bulkhead. The replica carving has been done in plaster.

Bottom left and right: Various details of the ornate decoration of the dining saloon. Captain James Cook and Horatio, Lord Nelson are just two of the well-known seamen and explorers depicted within escutcheons over the doorways in the side lobbies. The others are Francis Drake, John Franklin, Matthew Flinders, George Vancouver, George Anson and Jean-François La Pérouse.
The modern Corinthian capitals are made of plaster. Painted decoration is incorporated within the plaster scroll work.

Right: The Victorian water closet (a modern replica), carrying the royal coat of arms, is not original to the ship, but introduced for today's visitors. The original facilities can be found on the port side of the promenade deck.

THE FORWARD HOLD

Here can really be seen the details of the design of *Great Britain*'s innovative structure. Brunel and his team, with little previous experience of iron ship-building, nonetheless built a strong and seaworthy ship. For example, Brunel had reasoned that the main stresses in a seaway would be in the upper deck and the ship's bottom, and this latter is where you find the necessary structure to carry these stresses, with much evidence of careful detail design. Strangely perhaps Brunel didn't consider a complete upper deck in iron as necessary.

Later in life, *Great Britain* was to suffer as a result of being first in her field, for when it came to consider her for classification by Lloyds, a measure that didn't exist at the time of her build, her unique structure made it quite impossible for the classification society to fit her into their criteria for an iron ship. It was this issue that was partly responsible for her change, in the final phase of her career, to a sail-driven cargo ship.

Right: The modern ducting for the air conditioning, and the safety rails for the visitors' viewing platform, are visible on the right. The vast volume of this impressive space would not have been visible originally, as it was subdivided into two decks of accommodation and two of cargo holds. It has been left as found in the Falklands to allow the visitor an opportunity to view the ironwork and gain an impression of the ship's revolutionary structure.

The massive timbers visible in the middle of the hold formed the step, or footing, of the foremast after her conversion to a three-masted ship. Known as a mast partner, it transferred the weight of the mast into the strength members of the double bottom, and as her masts were probably the largest ever fitted to a sailing ship the mast partner is similarly large.

Right: Part of the reconstructed tank deck, the lowest, and the space where originally cargo and coal was stored and bunkered. In the present configuration it shows how the deck might have looked when *Great Britain* was converted as a troop transport for the Crimea in 1855. More than 300,000 troops from Britain, France and Turkey were transported and only the British merchant marine had the capacity for such an undertaking.

Opposite top: Two cavalry horses and a barrel of vinegar; rubbing horses down with vinegar during the voyage calmed them down.

Below and below right: A closer look at the enormously strong 'egg-box' structure worked into the bottom of the ship. This would have been mainly plated over at the start of her career to form the double bottom.

Above: Detail of the remains of one of the original decks left in as a stiffener along the ship's side after conversion to a pure cargo-carrying sailing ship.

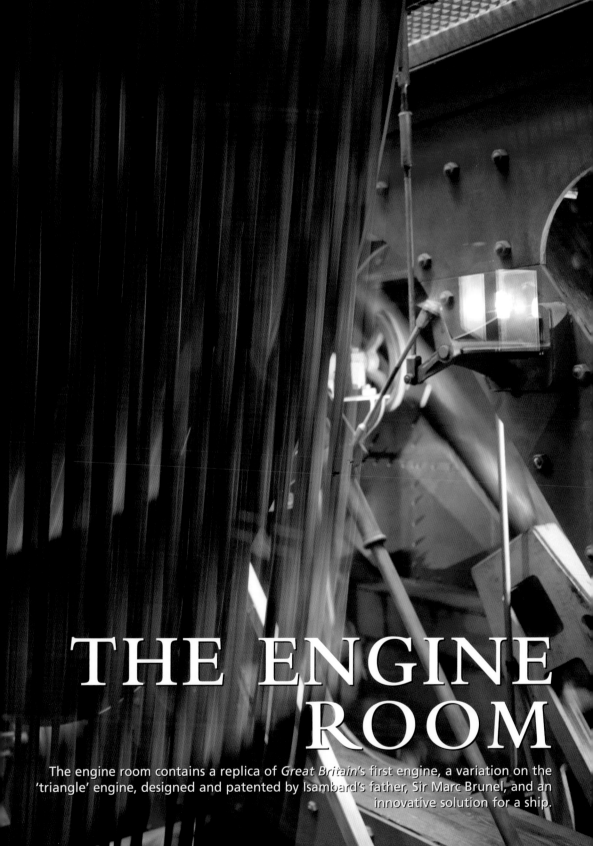

THE ENGINE ROOM

The engine room contains a replica of *Great Britain*'s first engine, a variation on the 'triangle' engine, designed and patented by Isambard's father, Sir Marc Brunel, and an innovative solution for a ship.

THE MAIN ENGINE, CHAIN DRIVE AND BOILERS ON view today are replicas commissioned after much careful research over the years. At the time of *Great Britain's* launch, it was the largest and most powerful marine engine ever to have been installed in a ship.

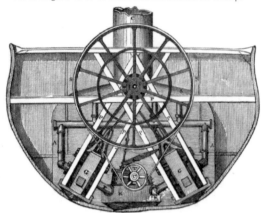

Left: A wheelbarrow containing ash from the boilers which would be transported up to the weather deck for disposal overboard.

Below: The hot and dirty work of stoking the boilers and removing the ash would have been carried out almost continuously when under steam. The steam was generated from seawater in a large rectangular boiler that was divided into three bays. It was stoked from both ends and had a total of twenty-four furnaces.

Right: One of the great cylinders can be seen on the left, while in the foreground are the bilge and hot water pumps.

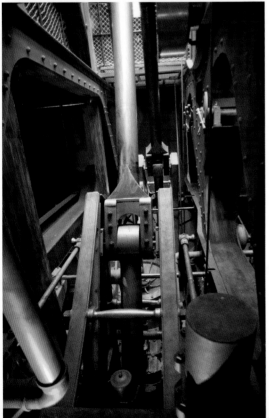

Opposite and above: General views of the engine seen through the chain drive. The heavy framework of the engine support, which can be seen in the background, was built into the ship's hull and was part of her basic structure. The massive main drive wheel at the top is 18ft 3in in diameter, while the smaller, lower drum is 6ft diameter. The propeller shaft, which is 18in diameter, was driven by the lower drum. The prominent disc-shaped objects are counter balances which counteract the valve piston and spindle so that steam pressure is not lost whilst transmitting into the main cylinders.

Left: A view on the top of one of the four cylinders, showing the connecting rod passing out of shot upwards to the massive crankshaft, which was water-cooled via a 10in hole drilled through it. Like so much of this engine, this crank was yet another huge feat of engineering, and it was forged by the Mersey Iron Works. To the right and left of this assembly can again be seen the great frames that supported the engine. There can be little doubt that when such a huge piece of machinery was operating it would have been felt and heard throughout the ship.

Above: At the level of the promenade deck is the control platform. Here is the starting wheel for controlling one pair of cylinders, either ahead or astern.

Left: Brunel's innovative belt drive that consisted of four separate chains weighing in total some 7 tons. The main drive wheel, driven off the engine crankshaft, had teak teeth with which to engage the chain; below, the propeller shaft drum, which suffered very heavy wear, had teeth of lignum vitae.

Below: The engine controls. Here the amount of steam to be let into the cylinders would be controlled via throttle valves installed in the main steam line out of sight and well below this position. The brass speaking trumpet conveyed orders from the navigating bridge on the weather deck.

Above: A view along the shaft of the so-called starting wheel which governed the direction the engine ran, either ahead or astern for the two cylinders immediately below the control position. It was mirrored at the other side of the main chain wheel by the starting wheel for the other two cylinders.

Left: Despite the apparent modernity of a steam engine, it was still partially dependent on something as traditional as tallow or rendered animal fat. This was used to lubricate bearings where steam would wash away other lubricants. Indeed, it continued to be used in this role until well into the twentieth century.

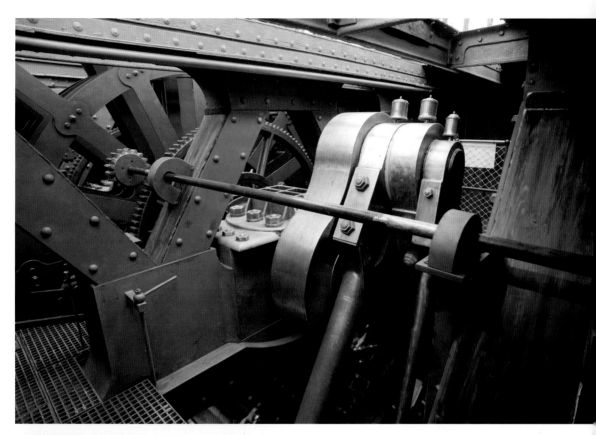

Left and above: Where tallow wasn't used, mineral or whale oil was. The brass covers are for oil pots to keep the bearings of the big ends lubricated. The view above shows the two upper pots on the cylinder connecting rod big ends and the lower one at the top of the air pump connecting rod.

Below, left: A set of spanners for the engineers.

Below, right: Two hand pumps positioned on the forward bulkhead of the engine room and arranged to pump brine off the top of the condensate in the condenser.

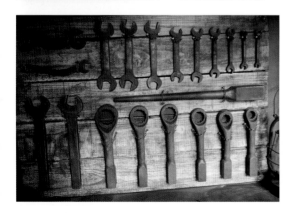

PRESERVING THE SHIP

The innovative system for ensuring *Great Britain*'s preservation, which involved the building of the 'glass sea', was put in place in 2004. Before that, the underwater hull, exposed to damp air, was rusting badly and the prognosis for the long-term survival of the ship was bleak.

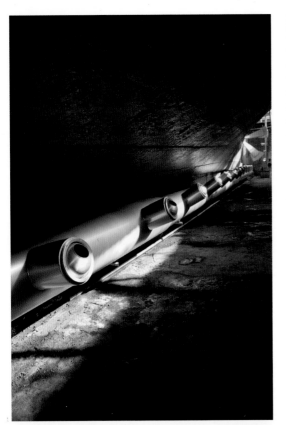

RESEARCH CARRIED OUT AT CARDIFF UNIVERSITY indicated that the wrought iron, saturated with salt, could be stabilised by the control of the humidity in and around the underwater hull of the ship. In normal conditions, damp and air promotes rusting; in a dry environment the sodium becomes inert. So, the 'glass sea' has a dual purpose: to encase the underwater part of the ship and at the same time emulate the surface of the sea.

Left: A view of the ducts for the lower hull's external dry air supply, arranged either side of the keel to create an upward flow of air, blanketing the iron plates and inhibiting the chloride corrosion that has proved so destructive.

Right: This striking view serves to illustrate the relatively fine lines of the ship as well as showing the modern paraphernalia needed to keep the underwater hull preserved. Visible here is the supporting structure of the 'glass sea' with the modern ventilation ducts, that extract the humid air as it rises, slung underneath.

Below: Deep inside the hull, away from public access, is the internal counterpart of the dry air ducting. A second demumidifier is located here and ducting from it runs around the ship between the iron hull and the cabin sides.

FURTHER READING

PUBLISHED SOURCES

Blake, Joe, *Restoring the Great Britain* (Redcliffe Press, 1989)

Brown, David K, 'The Introduction of the Screw Propeller into the Royal Navy', *Warship* no1 (Conway Maritime Press, 1977)

Brunel's SS Great Britain, Guidebook (SS *Great Britain* Trust 2009).

Corlett, Ewan, *The Iron Ship, the Story of Brunel's SS Great Britain* (Conway Maritime Press, second edition 1990)

Envig, Olaf T, *Viking to Victorian, Exploring the Use of Iron in Shipbuilding* (Themo Publishing, 2006)

Falconer, Jonathan, *What's Left of Brunel* (Dial House, 1995)

Fogg, Nicholas, *The Voyages of the Great Britain* (Chatham Publishing, 2002)

Greenhill, Dr Basil (ed), *Conway's History of the Ship: The Advent of Steam* (Conway Maritime Press, 1992)

Griffiths, Denis, *Steam at Sea: Two Centuries of Steam Powered Ships* (Conway Maritime Press, reprinted 2000)

————, *Brunel's 'Great Western'* (Patrick Stephens Limited, 1985)

————, Andrew Lambert and Fred Walker, *Brunel's Ships* (Chatham Publishing, 1999)

Lambert, Andrew, 'Brunel and the Screw Propeller', *Isambard Kingdom Brunel: Recent Works* (Design Museum, 2001)

Lavery, Brian, *SS Great Britain: An Insight into the Design, Construction and Operation of Brunel's Famous Passenger Ship: Owner's Workshop Manual* (J H Haynes, 2012)

Maddocks, Melvin (ed), *The Great Liners* (Time Life Publishing, 1978)

Morris, Chris, *The Great Brunel: A Photographic Journey* (Tanner's Yard Press, 2005)

Rolt, L T C, Isambard Kingdom Brunel (Penguin, 1990)

Young, Chris, *The Incredible Journey: The SS Great Britain Story 1970–2010* (SS *Great Britain* Trust, 2010)

The SS *Great Britain* Conservation Plan, 1999

Available from the SS *Great Britain* website www.ssgreatbritain.org/history/articles/

The conservation plan, published in 5 parts in 2 volumes

SELECTED WEBSITES

www.ssgreatbritain.org

www.ikbrunel.org.uk

www.cardiff.ac.uk/share/research/projectreports/ssgreat britain/index.html

www.nationalhistoricships.org.uk

THE BRUNEL INSTITUTE

The Brunel Institute, recently opened next to *Great Britain*, is open to members of the public on presentation of some form of identity. It houses material covering the history of the ship up to her return to Bristol in 1970. It also contains the David MacGregor Collection, which is made up of his extensive library relating to merchant sailing ships, his ship plans, photographs and research notes.

ACKNOWLEDGEMENTS

The publisher and authors would like to thank the staff of SS *Great Britain* for all their help in the production of this book, particularly Matthew Tanner, director of the SS *Great Britain* Trust, Keith Stanton, and Joanna Thomas.

All uncredited photographs in this book are by Herb Schmitz.